Crystal for Beginners

A Beginners Guide to Program Your Healing Crystals and Stones and Manifest Your Desires

Gabriel Davidson

Table of Contents

Introduction 4

Chapter 1: How crystals can help improve your life 10

Chapter 2: *The Energy of the Crystals* 15

Chapter 3: *Crystal Healing Properties* 31

Chapter 4: *Choosing the Right Crystal* 36

Chapter 5: *Purchasing and Caring of Crystals* 45

Chapter 6: *Benefits of Crystal Healing* 52

Chapter 7: *Healing Chakras with Crystals* 60

Chapter 8: *How to use crystals* 71

Chapter 9: *Programming methods* 76

Chapter 10: *Becoming Conscious of Crystals* 89

Chapter 11: *Recommended Crystals for Beginners* 105

Chapter 12: *Frequently asked questions* 112

Conclusion 116

Introduction

Crystals have been around for millions of years and have played an important role in human culture since prehistoric times. With their dazzling colors and unusual shapes and textures, they must have looked like something out of this world, and it's hardly surprising why they were used for magic, religious ceremonies, and initiations.

How early man managed to figure out their healing properties we'll never know, but a lot of what we know about the use of crystal in healing and magic comes from ancient Egypt. They may not have been the first to discover these properties but were the first to record them for posterity.

Since 500,000 BC, when the oldest clear quartz tools were discovered in a cave near Beijing, crystals have been part of our everyday life, in one way or another. Although our knowledge about crystals has grown and they've become an indispensable component of high-tech programs, our fascination with their magical and healing powers has not diminished.

On the contrary, objects of great beauty and powerful healing tools whose impact on the human body and psyche we are only beginning to understand, crystals continue to fascinate us. It was only relatively recently we realized that healing takes place not only on a physical but also on emotional and spiritual levels.

In the magic of crystals lies their ability to pick up vibrations from their environment and, in the case of negative energy, transform it into something positive and good. In the case of positive energy, they can amplify it to benefit all those who happen to find themselves in such an environment.

Ancient knowledge and practice we so easily renounced as legends and old wives' tales are things we are now struggling to restore and bring back to life. Unfortunately, much of it has been irretrievably lost. Still, as more and more people struggle to cope with the increasing stress and uncertainty of the modern world, the need for ancient wisdom is more important than ever.

The ancient Greeks asked the big questions about what it means to live a good life, and some of their theories on ethics and happiness have been backed by modern science. Let's hope the shift in human consciousness, which is underway, will help restore the place crystals once held in human culture.

The use of crystals and gemstones became prevalent in ancient Greece, and most of the crystal names we use today originate from that era. Even the word "crystal" comes from the Greek word *krustallos,* meaning "ice." They used this word because the people believed that crystals were ice frozen so solidly that they would never melt. Different crystals were often associated with the gods and used in religious rituals and to decorate their temples. The Greeks also had many superstitions that involved crystals, such as wearing amethyst to avoid getting drunk or having a hangover or rubbing hematite (a crystal associated with Ares, the god of war) all over their bodies before battle, believing it would make them invulnerable from then on.

Most religious texts such as the Koran and the Bible refer to crystals and gemstones several times. Many religious rituals incorporate crystals or assign a significant meaning to certain types of crystals. In many cultures, green stones were a symbol of life, and people were often buried with one of these stones over their hearts.

The Chinese culture has always emphasized jade, recognizing it as a kidney healing stone, and around 1,000 years ago, emperors were often buried in jade armor. Instruments in the form of chimes were commonly made and hung in homes and places of business, and even some of the characters in Chinese writing were designed to resemble jade beads.

Crystals no longer have such a deep cultural significance as they used to, though they are still a powerful tool for healing and improving the lives of those who use them. Some of the symbolism connected with stones is still incorporated into modern culture in small ways, especially in books and films, such as a green stone being a core element of restoring life to a dying world or returning a broken-off shard to a magical crystal that keeps the world in balance. Crystals are also still a popular subject for scientists to study, and there are many educational courses and professional careers that concern the use of crystals and their abilities.

Types of Crystals

1. Solid Crystals

Except for glass and amorphous substances, whose structure doesn't appear orderly but disorganized, all solid matter is formed during a crystalline state. Generally, it's presented as an aggregate of small crystals (or polycrystalline) like ice, very hard rocks, bricks, concrete, plastics, very proportional metals, bones, etc., or poorly crystallized because the wood fibers run.

They can even be single crystals of small dimensions like sugar or salt, valuable stones, and most minerals, some of which are utilized in modern technology for today's sophisticated applications, like quartz of oscillators or semiconductors of Electronic devices.

2. Luminous crystals

Some anisotropic liquids (see anisotropy), sometimes mentioned as "liquid crystals," are literally to be considered as mesomorphic bodies, that is, intermediate states of matter between the amorphous state and crystalline state.

Liquid crystals are utilized in displays of electronic devices. Its commonest design consists of two sheets of metallic glass that cover a thin film of mesomorphic substance. The appliance of an electrical tension to the film causes intense turbulence that involves an area diffusion of sunshine, with which the charged area becomes opaque. When the thrill disappears, the liquid regains its transparency. The properties of crystals, like their freezing point, density and hardness, are determined by the sort of forces that hold the particles together. They're classified into ionic, covalent, molecular, or metallic bonds.

3. Ionic Crystals

Ionic crystals have two important characteristics: they're formed of charged bonds, and therefore the anions and cations are usually of various sizes. They're hard and, at an equivalent time, brittle. The force that holds them together is electrostatic. Examples: KCl, $CsCl$, ZnS, and CF_2. Most ionic crystals have a high melting point, reflecting the good cohesion force that holds ions together. Its stability depends partially on its reticular energy; the higher this energy, the more stable the compound will be.

4. Covalent Crystals
The atoms of covalent crystals are held together during a three-dimensional network only by covalent bonds. Graphite and diamond, allotropes of carbon, are good examples. Thanks to its strong covalent bonds in three dimensions, the diamond features a particular hardness and a high freezing point. Quartz is another example of a covalent crystal. The distribution of silicon atoms in quartz is analogous to that of carbon in diamond, but in quartz, there's an oxygen atom between each pair of silicon atoms.

5. Molecular Crystals
During a molecular crystal reaction, the reticular points are occupied by molecules held together by Van der Waals forces and/or hydrogen bonds. The sulfur dioxide (SO_2) is an example of a solid molecular crystal to the likes of crystals of I_2, P_4, and S_8. Except for ice, molecular crystals are usually packed as close as their shape and size allow. Because Van der Waals forces and hydrogen bonds are weaker than ionic or covalent bonds, molecular crystals tend to be brittle, and most melt at temperatures below 100 ° C.

6. Metal Crystals
The metal crystals' structure is easier because each reticular point of the crystal is occupied by an equivalent metal atom. Metal crystals usually have a cubic structure centered on the body or faces; they will even be compact hexagonal packaging so that they are usually very dense. Its properties vary consistently with the species and range from soft to hard and with melting points from low to high, but it is generally a good conductor of warmth and electricity.

Chapter 1:
How crystals can help improve your life

Crystal healing is an alternative medicine technique that uses crystals and other stones to heal and protect against illness. The proponents of this technique believe that crystals act as channels for healing. So positive energy of healing can flow into the body when the heat that causes illness has shed.

Even though crystal healing has become more and more popular in recent years, this alternative treatment is not popular with most doctors and scientists, many of which are called crystal healing pseudoscience. Scientifically, there is no evidence that crystal healing can cure disease, as the condition is not the result of so-called energy flow in the body. Moreover, scientific studies have not shown that crystals and gems can be distinguished by chemical composition or color to treat certain diseases.

Nevertheless, Healing Crystals are famous in health spas and New Age Health Clinics and may have been incorporated into related massage and reiki practices. The use of crystals in such an environment may contribute to relaxation, but this effect is not supported by scientific knowledge either.

How it works

Crystal healing advocates believe that crystals and gems have healing-promoting properties. Many places that promote crystal healing have an ancient history of this practice, dating back at least 6,000 years to the classical Sumerian era of Mesopotamia. Ancient Egyptians prevented sickness and negative energy by decorating themselves with crystals such as lapis lazuli, carnelian, and turquoise. However, the modern philosophy of crystal healing is based on the traditional concepts of Asian culture, particularly the idea of Chinese life energy (Qi) and the Hindu or Buddhist chakra concept. This eddy of life energy connects the physical and supernatural elements of the body.

In crystal healing, stones been have assigned different properties, but healers have different ideas about which stones have which feature. For example, amethyst is considered by some to be beneficial to the intestine. Green Aventurine helps the heart. Yellow Topaz guarantees mental clarity. Red to purple colors have been connected to the seven chakra points on the body.

During a treatment session, a crystal healer can place various stones and crystals aligned to these chakra points roughly on the head area, forehead, neck, chest, and stomach to the intestinal and the genital regions. The stones used and their placement can be selected depending on the symptoms reported by the patient. All this has been influenced by the healer's knowledge and beliefs about the sick chakra philosophy and energy imbalances. Practitioners of Western medicine have mostly rejected this philosophy.

Crystal healing also includes the use of crystals and stones that can be worn on the body or placed under a pillow to drive off illness, drive away negative energy, or absorb positive energy. Talismans are labeled "amulets."

Actual mechanism

There are no scientific studies on the effectiveness of crystal healing, but one research suggests that crystal healing may have a placebo effect in patients undergoing this type of treatment. "The placebo effect is treatment-related, not directly related to the procedure itself that affects the patient's disease," said Christopher French, director of the Department of Abnormal Psychology at the University of London.

"There is no evidence that crystal healing works beyond the placebo effect," French told Live Science. "This is a good criterion for determining any form of treatment, but whether crystal healing or another type of [complementary and alternative medicine] is completely worthless depends on your placebo effect. It depends on your attitude."

As French emphasized, there are many treatments known to have no therapeutic effect other than placebo. Although these treatments may temporarily make you feel better, there is no evidence that they can cure the disease or cure any health problems. French says that if you have a severe medical problem, you should seek treatment from a qualified doctor rather than an alternative therapist.

Is Crystal Healing Safe?
Crystal healers become healers by passing accredited courses offered online by universities and "natural medicine" clinics, many of which are not centrally authorized. Currently, there are no state or federal laws explicitly regulating or standardizing the conduct of Crystal Healing or the licensing of Crystal Healers. In some states, this type of alternative treatment falls into the category of massage or body therapy. In these states, crystal healers may need to be licensed to practice.
Non-profit organizations such as the National Certification Board for Therapeutic Massage and Bodywork (NCBTMB) are also conducting voluntary committee certification tests for massage therapists and alternative therapists. NCTMB supports schools and companies that qualify alternative therapists only if they meet specific criteria set by the organization.

How To Choose a Crystal

When choosing a crystal for your personal use, have at least two of each primary color to use. This includes red, orange, yellow, green, blue, purple, pink, white, transparent, and black. Crystal color is associated with the chakra Center and may be associated with some illnesses. It has been recommended that you keep various crystals and gems at hand when working. My personal favorites at hand are Peridot, Hematite, Red Jasper, Rose Quartz, Rhodonite, Carnelian, Topaz, Amber, Tiger Eye, Malachite, Bloodstone, Moss Agate, Turquoise, Aquamarine, Lapis Lazuli, Amethyst, Fluorite, Clear quartz, moonstone, onyx, black tourmaline, and smoky quartz.

There are many crystals and gems, so don't be overwhelmed or confused when choosing the one that suits you. The best guide to choosing a crystal is to follow intuition. When you listen to it, your intuition will never mislead you. Even if you haven't worked with the "intuition" instinct before, listening to it when using it can be challenging to understand. When choosing a new crystal, make sure it feels good, and you are happy. You don't want to attract negative, energetic emotions, so put some lively music in your car and think about what you enjoy when you head to the glass shop. When you get there, start looking around and see if anything catches your eye first. Pick up the crystal and see if it suits you. If so, search for more to add to your crystal healing kit. If not, leave and move it to another location! There is no right or wrong answer, but what resonates with you? Remember that your crystals choose you as much as you choose them!

Chapter 2:
The Energy of the Crystals

The title of this chapter asks an important question. Just exactly why is it any of us should be worrying about or using healing crystals? The answer to this particular question is not exactly hard to answer. You will find that there are many different answers to this question plastered all over the internet. But the plethora of answers also brings with it a problem: Which are right?

Unfortunately, this isn't one of those issues which has a single simple answer. There is no one reason to use healing crystals. There are dozens upon dozens. Some of these uses seem to go together quite well and make it easy to see how they interact with each other. But then there are those answers which seemingly contradict other answers. If you believe that there is one solid answer as to why you should use healing crystals, you will wind up somewhat frustrated with the whole ordeal.

To give this question enough room to be properly answered, I have collected together many different reasons people use healing crystals. These range from seeking balance and calming the emotions to stepping out of the electromagnetic field, finding pain relief, romance, or even detoxifying your home. You'll notice that these range from purely psychological to entirely mystical. I'd like to give you a full understanding of the topic rather than one that simply dismisses or wholly embraces the mystical realm. Each of us has our own spiritual beliefs and ideals. Rather than try to convince you of a spiritual concept, this approach will let you investigate it for yourself to decide if crystal healing is right for you or not.

Getting in Touch With Your Emotions.
Many of us go through life as a slave to our emotions. If we are happy, then we think that life is wonderful, but when we're sad or anxious, we think that life is horrible, that it only wants to hurt us, and that it never did anything good for anyone. If you believe in chakras, you may see this as a sign that your chakras

are clogged up, but most people don't have this disconnection from their own emotional experience. Instead of seeing their emotions as something that *happens* to them, they see emotions as an intrinsic part of themselves. We all tend to do this, to over-identify with our emotions instead of regarding them as transient phenomena. Getting lost in our emotions can be very scary, but healing crystals can help us out a lot in this area.

Different crystals have different purposes; some help with romance, those that help with pain, some that help to calm us, and some that improve our concentration. We'll be looking at these in more depth, but the range of uses points towards our emotional experiences. How can we be calm if we are lost in our emotions? As we'll see, we can turn to a healing crystal.

Regardless of how you use your crystals, one of the powerful things about them is how they take on meanings of their own. For example, we use amethyst to help us deal with our anxiety or sadness. If we find that we are overly irritable, then we'll use some jade. If we have too much stress, we can use the gorgeous moonstone to help us let go. These are just a few of the available crystals we use for emotional purposes, but how do they help us?

We'll be using the word intention a lot throughout the book. For our purposes right now, an intention is simply the purpose that we want our crystals to serve. If you are stressed, you would take a moonstone and set the intention as stress relief. As you gather more crystals around you, you'll come to have one or two each for most of your emotions that you need help dealing with. When you feel the negative emotion, you then turn to your healing crystals rather than get lost in them. Whether it is the crystal itself or the intention you set, which helps you deal with the feeling, the result is the same. You create a space between yourself and your emotional experience and then use crystals to alter and change it.

Practicing with healing crystals is a fantastic way to learn more about your emotions. They also offer a wonderful way of getting in touch with your reactions and responses. First, you need to identify that you are upset before turning to your healing crystals to help you manage it. This act of identifying your emotional experience is one of the most effective ways of understanding your emotions and conquering them.

Seek Balance
If you believe in chakras, you know that they are situated throughout your body, and each one acts almost like a gate. If they are open, then healing energy can flow through them. When your chakras are open, you have a great sense of peacefulness and contentment. But problems start to occur when they get closed or blocked up. If you believe in their significance, most of the emotional and mental problems we experience are explained through chakras.

Everything in the world is made up of frequencies, primarily electromagnetic, and crystals are no different here. However, different crystals have different frequencies, which makes them better or worse for a particular use. We are said to have seven different chakras, and each of these reacts to a different frequency. We might have problems in our lower chakra and find that we can't find romance or sexual fulfillment. Or we might have a problem with our throat chakra and discover that we never speak up for ourselves, ask the questions we need to know or speak in a manner that touches the depths of our inner being. When this is the case, we can turn to different crystals. For example, we might wear a necklace with lapis lazuli to unblock our throat chakra.

If you find that you feel like you are out of balance in your life and mind, you may want to consider exploring your chakras. A healing crystal could help you in this matter so that you can live your life as the most activated and honest version of yourself possible.

Romance and Sexual Energy

Both romance and sexual energy have chakras assigned to them. Romance is located in the heart, while sexual energy or potency is found in the lower regions just above the genitals. These are two of the spaces which are said to get blocked up the most often. When we are unlucky in love, we can often convince ourselves that we were meant to be alone or that our loneliness is a sign of our worthlessness. There is nothing wrong with a relationship ending or a date going poorly; this is simply the risk involved in any interpersonal relationship. But when we convince ourselves that our love life is a sign of something wrong with us, we clog up our chakras. Or, if you don't believe in chakras, you might interpret this as the way we can get lost in our thoughts and allow our negativity to spiral out and affect our lives.

One use for healing crystals is to help repair this damage in our hearts. To help us deal with matters of romance, we use a crystal with a pink, orange, or red color. This color alone connects it to the same emotional sphere as love, which helps us fuse our intentions into the crystal and our minds. We may choose to wear a low-hanging necklace to keep our healing crystals over our hearts and allow its vibrational frequencies to be closest to our love chakra.

Another issue that we often face is thinking that we are sexually repulsive or too unqualified to pleasure another being. While we might not have much experience, there is no reason that we should feel this way. When two people come together, they need to discover each other's bodies themselves to learn how they work. This is a process filled with errors and mistakes and (hopefully) laughter and love. But we live in a society that tells us how well we should perform, when we should have sex, how long we should have it for, and all sorts of other weird messages that lead to confusion and result in us getting bewildered and lost. Rather than live in the experience and enjoy it for what it is, we burden ourselves with anxiety, worries, and nervousness. These can greatly reduce how pleasurable the experience is for both parties.

By infusing a healing crystal with sexual energy, we can break free from the messages we have been told and, instead, get back in touch with the act itself. You may want to meditate with your crystal before performing, or you may want to wear it on a bracelet or something similar. By setting your intention ahead of time, connecting with this crystal becomes a way of tapping into the limitless libido inside of us all.

It should be noted that healing crystals used for matters of love don't just refer to the type of romantic love between two people. These crystals can also be a great way to get in touch and rediscover a love for yourself. If you are having a hard time accepting who you are or don't love yourself yet, then a healing crystal with the intention of love might be exactly what you need.

Improve Psychic Powers

You don't need to be a psychic to get benefits from using healing crystals. This is a common myth in practices that have come to be known as the new age. The perfect example of this is tarot cards, as they are one of the most widely known of these practices. But just like tarot cards, healing crystals are more often used for the psychological benefits that they provide rather than psychic ones. Like tarot cards, healing crystals can be used for psychic purposes, though this is not their most common use. It is like using a spoon as a fork, it can do what you want, but it wasn't intended for this purpose.

Those with psychic powers may use amethyst or apophyllite to activate and strengthen their third eye, that psychic eye that exists inside the forehead and the brain. The crystals are given the intention of improving your psychic abilities. They are typically worn as part of a decorative headband or placed on the forehead during meditation. The vibrations from these crystals help open up and clear out the third eye so that your psychic visions will be more powerful.

Improve Your Skin

While some aren't especially bothered, most of us want to have beautiful and healthy-looking skin clear from blemishes and other unattractive features. The populations of affluent countries spend millions upon millions of dollars on skincare products, not just every year but every single quarter. New products come out all the time with the latest scientifically formulated mixture to ensure that your skin looks lovely. But, instead of turning to these endlessly new creations, perhaps we could benefit from turning towards something a little bit older and more natural. It has been this idea that has driven the market of healing crystals used in skincare products.

There have been quite a few products of late that use small pieces of crystal to ensure beautiful skin. One example is the Gemstone Organic Rose Quartz Creme, which uses rose quartz and smoky quartz, and kunzite. Another product is the Tracie Martyn Complexion Savior, which includes a little bit of malachite. Of course, it should be clear that these use healing crystals as part of their overall product and not as the product itself. This brings into question whether or not the crystals have anything to do with improving the skin at all. It could just be that the pharmaceutical ingredients do all the work.

In that case, what about a face roller that uses jade? These have been around for quite some time, and they are known to help reduce the puffy appearance of skin. Not only that, but they leave a noticeable shine to the skin that suggests that they help bring the natural oils to the surface. This is further backed up by the fact that jade rollers help the skin absorb creams and other rub-on products. That's made possible by the way jade helps to open the pores of the skin. Next time you are thinking about purchasing some facial cream or other skin care products, consider adding healing crystals to your routine.

Help Plants Grow

This is one of the many uses that healing crystals have around the house. Some people like to bring healing crystals into the home for decorative purposes, but others use them more thoughtfully. This particular use stands outside of any science that I know of, including that of the placebo effect. Simply put, plants don't have the neurological component necessary for the placebo effect to work. It may be that adding crystals to a plant provokes the placebo effect in the owner, as they see the crystal as doing the work rather than the plant's environment and biology. But when looking for more information on this particular use, it becomes clear that it is tightly tied to psychic explanations.

There is a tendency to think of psychics as having the ability to see into the future or perceive possible threads of fate as they are weaved together. This is most obviously jokes made at the expense of psychics, such as "If you're psychic, then you should know who's calling." But what this misses is that a psychic isn't necessarily able to see into the future, so much as they work from and through emotions, intuition, and other unseen elements of understanding. One of the things that are often reported is that psychics have a strong connection to nature, or they have an intuitive sense as to the needs of Mother Nature. It is this connection that leads us to the use of healing crystals in raising plants.

Crystals are added to the soil or the container housing the plant. The plant's vibrational frequencies should be in the same range as the crystal. This needs to be discovered intuitively, and some psychics suggest asking your plants which crystals they want to use. Add the crystal and watch as the plant begins to thrive.

Aid in Feng Shui

Chakras are one way to explain and understand the emotional and spiritual experiences that we are having as we go about our lives. They play on the unseen energies that affect and move us all. Each of us is a world unto ourselves, which means that we bring our energies with us no matter where we go. But there is also environmental energy, unseen forces that lend power to the places we occupy. If you have ever walked into a room and immediately felt negative energy, then you know first-hand how locations can take on and store their own emotional and intangible vibrational energy.

One way that we cleanse and balance these environmental energies is through the use of feng shui. Rather than living at odds with the environmental energy around us, feng shui gives us a way of smoothing out our experience so that the energy of the environment and the energy we bring can coexist without clashing. Feng shui practices range from the way you position furniture to how often you clean your windows, as well as what objects you bring into the house. Some of the objects that we can use to increase our feng shui are healing crystals.

These stones represent a form of energy taken from the earth. They are energy collected into a physical form that you can then use with care and consideration to assist in your life and your feng shui. Just as these crystals can be used to balance our emotions, they can help us balance the energies of our home. But to this end, we must keep in mind that each crystal has a different purpose and power. It doesn't help our feng shui out if all we do is place crystals around the house in a haphazard and unconsidered manner. If you were placing heaters in your house, you wouldn't just place them anywhere. You would consider each room and where the best location to put them is and how much heat you need in a particular space. Healing crystals should be used in this manner, considered, and placed carefully to achieve an effect rather than left to the chaos of indifference.

The most commonly used crystal in feng shui is the jade crystal. This crystal is said to bring good luck to the owner and make the home into a luckier space. It is commonly paired with the money bonsai as a gift since both are meant to bring riches. It also represents the possibility of new beginnings, so it is a particularly great crystal, to begin with, in the sense of starting to use crystals as a beginning in and of itself. Also used often is clear quartz, which helps to remove the negative energies from around the home. Rose quartz is also quite popular since it represents love. If you are married, then rose quartz is used to help strengthen the relationship and create loving energy in the home. Remember that these are just a few examples of how healing crystals are used in feng shui. I'm sure you'll discover plenty more yourself.

Pain Relief

Pain can cripple us and steal away our lives. Or, at least, it can make it feel that way. If you experience chronic pain, then you know first-hand how debilitating it can be. You might have a thousand things you need to get done, but if you're in too much pain, then there's no way you're going to get out of bed. If you experience anything that brings a lot of pain into your reality, then you've probably looked for ways to treat it. While modern medicine has achieved wonders in this field, there is still a lot of work that needs to be done. I can't begin to tell you how many people I've met have been prescribed opiates despite not wanting them. It seems that our primary way of dealing with pain is through dangerously addictive chemical concoctions. I don't want to suggest that these have no value, but they have many negative side effects, which discourages many people from using them.

Healing crystals offer us another way of dealing with our pain, and there are tons of people who swear by them. Whether it was their natural frequencies that helped out or it was the placebo effect, the fact of the matter is that many people have found pain relief through using crystals. They are not the kind of thing that would be recommended by doctors, but they can help. Rather than claim them to be better or worse than medication, please make sure you seek out a professional medical opinion in conjunction with their use rather than relying solely on the crystals. With that said, let's take a quick look at some of the crystals that people use to take their lives back from pain.

Amethyst is often called the master healer, and it is considered the most effective crystal in treating pain. It has a very high frequency of vibration that makes it appropriate for treating pains such as arthritis or headaches. It is also used to treat stress. Cortisol, the stress hormone, can make the pain worse, so this is doubly beneficial. Lapis lazuli is also recommended for pain relief, though it only has minor healing properties that make it best for smaller pains. What lapis lazuli has going for it is the fact that it helps to strengthen the mind, which can make us better at withstanding the pain. Hematite is used to help with the flow of blood through the body, and it is worn to reduce blood pressure and other issues that can make your veins feel like they are filled with fire. Rose quartz is used in the treatment of skin, not only as a cosmetic but also to reduce the pain from burns and inflammatory issues. If you've got a sunburn, use a little rose quartz along with your aloe vera to help lower the level of pain overall.

Increase Your Happiness
We already talked about how healing crystals can help you get in touch with your emotions. This same feature has a bi-product of helping you to understand your happiness in a much fuller sense. But this isn't the only way in which healing crystals improve and increase our happiness. Many different crystals are said to have healing powers, and we'll briefly look at those, but first, there is a more mundane consideration we need to take into account. Simply put: crystals are attractive.
One of the reasons that crystals became so popular was because of their gorgeous and serene looks. They can have bold, bright colors, or they could be clear or even entirely dark. Some shine; others let light pass through them. They all have different textures and feelings, and these can make them quite enjoyable to hold in your hand. The beautiful nature of these crystals tends to spark reflection and bring the mind into a

pleasant state as you consider their beauty. One of the best things we can do for our happiness is take in beautiful things such as nature or art, and crystals are another of these beautiful objects we can use to improve our sense of wellbeing. Moving on from crystals as a whole, we find many different healing crystals have ties to the emotional sphere of happiness. The amazonite is said to bring joy through how it helps us discover and listen to our inner thoughts and feelings. We each have an inner truth, a way that we want to live. This isn't the same as an ambition like, "I want to be a successful writer or actor." Instead, this is more like, "I want to be a good person and to bring positivity to those around me." This is a deeper truth. Unfortunately, we often have a hard time connecting to such truths, and thus we live our lives as we are told we should and not as we genuinely want to deep inside. Amazonite can help us to connect to this truth. In doing so, it helps us live more honestly and fully and appreciate those around us, as well as ourselves.

Citrine is a beautiful, bright yellow crystal. If we look at citrine, it is hard not to think of the sun and the brightness of day or the warm feeling from bathing in its rays. This stone brings a feeling of being carefree and makes us more likely to take actions that put us outside of our comfort zone. While this may sound uncomfortable, psychologists have discovered that we are happiest when trying new things and pushing ourselves to achieve more.

Tiger eye is another crystal with connotations of nature and the sun. Its tiger-striped colors, with lots of brown, evokes a lovely feeling of nature, of the forests and trees that provide us with our oxygen and thus our ability to live in the first place. This helps us tap into that primal center inside of us all so that we can find strength and courage to take on whatever life throws at us.

You might be noticing a pattern with these three crystals. While some are said to bring happiness directly, many crystals don't do this. What they do is to help bring balance across each section of our lives so that we can more easily find happiness. They help us reduce our stress so that we can live happier and push us to be more inventive and energetic. They help us to tap into our internal strength so that we can discover more about ourselves. All these are avenues to find happier lives. They don't directly affect happiness, but they affect the factors that positively contribute to happiness.

Tap Into Calmness

One of the things that have already begun to crop up frequently throughout this book is how our modern world isn't designed to facilitate our emotional needs. Nowhere is this more clear than when we look at the idea of calmness. Have you noticed how everything seems to happen faster and faster these days? We have a 24/7 news cycle, and our social media feeds never end; they just go on forever. Commercials are edited to overload our senses, and we're constantly fighting traffic jams, balancing our finances, and trying to get promoted. All of this tells us to go, go, go, but it doesn't consider what this is doing to our psyches. Our constant need to push forward and keep moving, keep aiming for what's next, keep up with the news, and stay active online all cause us lots of stress. We don't always notice that we have this stress because we're so bombarded with it that we've come to see it as normal.

But then it comes time for bed, and we find ourselves unable to sleep. We're restless. We've been told to go faster and faster, to do more and more, to take in more information. But we're never told to relax and calm down and take time away to get back in touch with ourselves, to seek out a piece of calm within us. This message has been so readily ignored that many of us think that calmness is a bad thing.

But if we want to live a healthy life, we need to find a calm center within ourselves. This will lower our anxiety, improve our happiness, and increase our life expectancies. But with so many of us unsure of how to go about it, it can be hard to achieve. Thankfully, there are healing crystals that can help us here.

Amethyst, hematite, and moonstone are just three types of healing crystals that help to create a sense of calm. Their energies are very mild. This doesn't mean that they aren't potent, but they help us in a way that isn't explosive or over the top. They do the exact opposite; they soothe us instead of stimulating us. These calming energies can be felt when worn as jewelry, but the most effective approach is to combine calming crystals with meditation or even a bath. These activities already help to promote a sense of calm that grows exponentially when combined with the use of a healing crystal picked and imbued for this purpose.

Protection from Negative Energies
One way to protect ourselves from negative energies is by seeking understanding and balance in our emotional realm. Another way is to use feng shui to make our living environment a more relaxed and positive place. But these are just two ways in which we bring positivity into our lives. To

use a stretched metaphor, this kind of protection is like purchasing a gun. It can bring with it a sense of protection, but it doesn't do anything to prevent intruders. Likewise, when we balance our emotions or use feng shui, we increase our happiness, but we aren't preventing the negative from entering our lives. To complete the metaphor, we don't need a gun. We need a fence.

We build a fence up around our happiness, and this protects us from negativity. We might still encounter negativity in our lives, but our fence keeps it at a distance. We aren't opening our doors and inviting it in. We can see it, recognize it for what it is, and then go back inside and continue to be content. Since we're talking about happiness and negativity, there are no real fences. But we can use healing crystals to give us an assist in this manner.

Some healing crystals are used for protection, such as fire agate, black obsidian, or fluorite. Adding these stones to your home or your jewelry can help to give you this protection. Whether the stones do it themselves or function on the placebo effect again, the result is the same. You become more aware of how you interact with negativity, which helps you distance yourself from it. Knowing that you are protected, you can see the negativity without looking through the eyes of fear.

If you want the most protection possible, then a bracelet or necklace with multiple crystals is the way to go. But don't just use stones that are meant for protection. Instead, use a protection stone and then a happiness stone, another protection stone, and a stone for health. By combining these, you create a piece of jewelry that not only protects you from negativity but actively invites positivity into your life as well.

Chapter 3:
Crystal Healing Properties

Crystals have been revered for the beauty and crystal healing effects. The Melbourne Art Gallery clarifies their geological origin, and numerous rooms have been allocated to flaunt crystals. Over time, the art of crystal healing has survived criticism from skeptics, so it is somewhat reassuring to see that the science of Geology holds them in such high regard to dedicate rooms in museums to them.

What I want to explain is the possibility that crystal recovery may work and endeavor to throw some light on why some people feel such a sense of healing and wellbeing after a crystal healing session.

Using explanation, let's go back to the science laboratory. We learned that everything is made up of atoms. Solids comprise of lots of atoms and look solid since the atoms are so dense (close together) that it looks strong. Dense materials with atoms are those even less dense,

Everything around us, including you and me, is composed of those atoms or even smaller particles oscillating (moving); however, we don't perceive how they proceed because our senses cannot pick up that.

Crystals can also be made up of these atoms and oscillate (move) at a specific pace. Studies have been done for the past 5 decades or more at UCLA to research this, and you can get these on the net.

The way that you move, feel and think, etc., is unique to you. There's no other person in this world that is a duplicate of you.

We become influenced by the vibrations of other people, and if you don't believe this, simply spend an hour listening to some friend on the telephone that feels down, and by the time they've run out of steam, and you put down the phone, you are feeling down also.

We are picking up other people's 'vibes' and enabling individuals to interact with our energy. In precisely the same way, the crystals and everything else about us has a vibration that defines a rose quartz crystal from topaz and so on.

Crystals are distinct in that they have a hierarchical arrangement of the atoms that differ. They oscillate (vibrate) differently, making them distinctive from their names, e.g., smokey quartz differs from amethyst effects when they come into close contact with every one of us.

Our vibration begins to move since the crystal is near us as we would become influenced around us.

This is a portion of the research I referred to earlier and readily available online. It is stated; as they interact with our vibrations, the crystals have a beneficial impact on people, our energy centers, and how our atoms oscillate alters.

If you consult the books about each crystal's qualities, there is much information on how they could affect you and how every crystal can cure different emotions, etc.

There is testimony enough for this to matter that they feel different after undergoing a crystal recovery.

While some people don't think, there has to be some reason why people feel different. Combine that with all the studies, and it becomes open to uncertainty as to if it could be just a placebo effect.

The healer places crystals required on or around the client's body or energy field. The client is usually lying down on a massage mattress or the ground. Ideal conditions are if the room is dim; there are candles along with some soft music or some nice smelling incense.

The notion is that the customer relaxes and lets the crystals do their job. The length of time it takes depends on the recovery that is needed.

It's stated that crystals change the method by which the energy centers, also known as chakras, vibrate. They undo emotional and energetic blockages in the energy field and the physical body.

New energy may enter by unblocking these, and it'll flow, enhancing life, health, and vitality.

So crystals are a tool for bringing healing and balance to the body, thoughts, emotions, and spirit. Whether it is for you or not can be determined, and your personal experience might be useful if you could try it on your own.

Don't expect that one or two healings will work wonders. It has taken you months, sometimes years of neglect of particular regions of your life, and there is no magic wand to whisk it away. That is life, not television, and recovery takes time.

Crystal Therapy for Ailments

Crystal therapy is a treatment that is used to give treatment for various ailments like pain and anxiety.

The quick pace lifestyle and working hours have given birth to diseases like stress and body pain. This is a technique that helps a lot in providing comfort. This therapy has been in use since time immemorial.

In crystal treatment, crystals and stones are widely used. It is believed that these crystals help in providing healing effects on the human body.

Some of the stones and crystals are thought to possess curative nature. These stones and crystals are put on an effective role to deliver an effect.

This healing treatment is essentially a science. There is no scientific evidence for this therapeutic technique.

But it's commonly utilized to provide a comforting effect. These crystals, when implemented on the skin, provides a calming effect.

The science behind this healing therapy is that it stimulates the skin cells. Then, this leads to the emission of enzymes and hormones that help in providing relaxation.

It's believed that the mother character owns a cure for various ailments. Various materials contain specific healing properties.

These crystals are employed to have a healing impact. These crystals are utilized to offer a rejuvenating effect.

The principle of crystal therapy is simple. On the body area affected by the pain, the stones and crystals are applied and used to massage.

These work on the energy grids of their body. The crystals are utilized to remove the negative and adverse energy.

Some experts are currently offering crystal therapy. Even though it hasn't been proven whether they have a healing impact or not.

However, the use of this therapy reflects its benefits. This treatment has contributed to health benefits. We cannot conclude that this treatment doesn't have some advantages.

You can use crystal therapy to get perfect relief from the pain. The stones and crystals have been put on different parts of the body, affected by the pain. This treatment is very effective in providing comfort.

Stones and the crystals in the form that is heated are placed to provide relaxation. The hidden healing power of the stones helps in taking away the stress and worry. This results in offering a soothing influence on the mind.

One interesting fact connected with crystal treatment is that it doesn't have any side effects.

This is a very effective technique which can reduce pain without supplying any side effect. Crystals and natural stones will enhance your health standards.

Chapter 4:
Choosing the Right Crystal

Being a newbie in the realm of crystal healing, one of the first lessons to learn is how to choose the right crystal for yourself and/or for the chosen purpose. The trick is this statement, 'You don't choose crystals. They choose you!'

Finding the Right Crystals in a Brick-and-Mortar Store Using Your Intuition

Typically, if you are looking at a set of crystals, and you feel drawn toward one of them, then it is usually a vibrational match for your energy frequency. Take your eyes away from the stone that you feel an initial attraction for and, after some time, look at it again and see how you feel.

Hover your dominant hand over the crystal or better still, hold it in your hand. Close your eyes and observe any subtle energy changes or vibrations you feel in your body. If you do, then this crystal is answering your needs. You can go ahead and choose it.

Remember that you may not always be able to discern the subtle vibrational changes in energy when you hold the crystal, especially as a beginner. In such cases, go ahead and make your choice based on your initial reaction. Use the crystal for a week or two, and observe your experiences. With patient practice, you will find it increasingly easy to discern energy changes regardless of how subtle they are.

So, regardless of what you want the crystal for, trust your gut instinct and play along with it. And one of the most valuable suggestions you can get is not to overthink excessively about your choice of crystals.

You don't need to study and research the different types of crystals available before making your choice. Choose what attracts you, and then do a bit of research. More often than not, you will see that your choice of crystal matches your needs.

Another piece of useful advice you can use is to take things slowly. First, take one crystal, use it for a week, and see how you feel and connect with its auric energy. Observe and make notes of the behavioral and attitudinal changes in your life, in yourself as well as those of others around. The changes are likely to be very subtle, and, therefore, you must focus a little more than normal on observing.

Once you are fine with what is happening, you can go back and choose more crystals for yourself.

Finding the Right Crystal in a Virtual Online Store Using Your Intuition

Nearly all virtual stores will have some basic information and pictures of the crystals for you to choose from. Look at one page of pictures, and see which one attracts you the most or on which of the crystals do your eyes linger.

Most often, the crystals you are attracted to in a particular situation are relevant in your life for that time. Instead of trying to find 'scientific and logical' reasons for your attraction, know and believe that your intuition is telling you what your soul needs. This is why you must trust your intuitive powers and go along with their calling.

Until now, you are focusing on the crystals you are drawn to. You can shift your perspective for a moment and focus on those crystals and gemstones that you feel repelled against. Those are the ones that you must avoid choosing then because your intuition is telling you that the vibrational energy of that crystal is not aligned to your present needs.

Receiving a Crystal as a Gift

Sometimes, people can choose crystals for you, and when this happens, remember that the crystal has chosen to be with you even without you stepping out to make your choice. The stone has found a way into your life through a caring friend. If you receive a crystal as a gift, then accept it wholeheartedly with an open mind in the same way you accepted your initial attraction to stone when you went shopping for your crystal.

However, receiving crystals as gifts usually comes at a later stage in your crystal collection journey. As you increasingly connect with crystals and through them to the universal power, your needs and desires are caught onto by the universe. Using the law of attraction, the universe finds a way to get your crystals delivered to your doorstep. Typically, such deep desires to have a particular crystal to achieve a particular purpose are realized in the form of gifts.

Taking this point in the reverse direction, suppose you lose a crystal. Yes, you will feel bad about losing it, and you could shed a few tears and be disappointed in yourself for being careless and not looking after your beloved stone well. However, you must remember that it is very likely that the stone has served its purpose in your life, and the universe has found a way to pass on the benefits of its power to someone else that needs it. So, just like how crystals find their way to you when you need them, they could go away from you when their purpose is served. Therefore, learn to let go if you lose anything in your life.

Choosing a Crystal Based on Its Properties

If you are looking for a crystal for a particular ailment or problem, you can find gemstones known to help in solving these problems. For example, there are specific crystals like aventurine that have vibrational energy suitable to boost confidence. So, if you are looking to build confidence, then you can choose an aventurine.

Aventurine is not the only stone that helps to boost confidence. Even crystals like bloodstone, carnelian, etc., are great for this problem. You can go through all the crystals based on a specific property you are looking for and then choose from among these using your intuition's guide.

Finding the Right Crystal Using the Pendulum Dowsing Method

Using the pendulum dowsing method is a bit of an advanced technique and requires you to have a bit of experience. Yet, even for a beginner, it makes sense to know how it works. Use the following steps for this method:

Find the right dowsing pendulum - Think about what kind of dowsing pendulum you would like to have. There are numerous crystal-based pendulums you can choose from, and you can make a simple one at home too. An easy-to-make do-it-yourself dowsing pendulum needs a tea bag or a favorite bead or a favorite crystal or stone tied to the end of a string.

Cleanse and clear the pendulum of negative energies. If you already have a pendulum that you use for your divination purpose, you might already know how to cleanse and clear your instrument.

Connect with and build a lasting relationship with your pendulum. You have to learn the pendulum's language and connect with it to build a lasting relationship with your divination instrument. This step is important to understand and catch the messages that your pendulum is trying to tell you every time you use it for divination purposes, including choosing the right crystal. Follow these steps to connect with your pendulum:

• Take a few deep breaths and ground yourself

•Seek support and help from the universe to help you achieve your purpose. You can use your prayers or ask in simple language for help.

- Ask your pendulum some basic questions to understand yes, no, or maybe answers it might choose to give. For this to work, remember to ask questions to which you already know the answers. Other ways of setting up a communication channel with your pendulum include:

Ask your pendulum, 'what is a yes?' and wait for the answer. It could move clockwise or counterclockwise. Make a note of this reply.

Next, ask your pendulum, 'What is a no?' or 'What is maybe?' and wait for the answers, and make suitable notes.

- Another way you can establish a communication channel with your pendulum is by getting responses to questions like:
  - Am I male or female?
  - Is it right that I am [fill in your age] old?
  - Are my eyes brown?
  - Do I enjoy reading?

The yes/no answers given by your pendulum will help you know how your pendulum is connecting with you.

Now, your pendulum is ready for use. Place your chosen crystal on a table and hold your pendulum over it. Watch for the signs given by your divination instrument and make your choice of whether you want to take this crystal or not. Your divination pendulum is a great tool to help you make many choices.

Other Elements of the Crystal to Focus On

While being guided by your feelings and intuition is the best way to choose your crystals, here are some more elements you should focus on while making your choice:

Form of the crystal - Typically, most crystals emit their power through the edges, and the most intense power comes from their tips. The form of the crystal you choose depends on its use. A stone with multiple edges and splintered tips will radiate and emit its energy through all the edges and tips. However, the energy radiation may not be uniform when you use crystals with this form.

Spheres, on the other hand, radiate their energy uniformly. However, the radiation from a spherical-shaped crystal will be weaker than when emitted through an edge. Usually, crystals that are cut to a specific shape tend to have more radiation power, while tumbled stones tend to radiate energy more gently, softly, and harmoniously than other forms.

Quality of the crystal - Stones that display a particular crystal's unique characteristics are of better quality than those that don't display the expected traits. For example, the quality of clear quartz is determined by its brightness. The more cloudy it is, the lesser the quality of the clear quartz.

On the other hand, a transparent ruby is more powerful than an opaque one. And yet, you must remember that the looks and profile of stone are less important than its potential power. Follow your gut feeling here too, and even if you feel a stone is not what it appears, but your intuition powers are on a high when you hold it, then the crystal could be right for you. Remember that sometimes crystals simply need cleansing and cleaning to regain their original luster.

Size of the crystal - The larger the crystal's size, the more power it can radiate. A small-sized amethyst will radiate power only to a short range of distance, whereas a big druse or collection of amethyst crystals can radiate power to cover an entire room. Therefore, you must choose the size of your crystal based on your needs.

For example, if you want to place a stone to radiate its power to clear the negative energies from a big room, then you must choose a large-sized crystal or maybe even a cluster of crystals. However, if you want to wear a crystal around your neck, you can choose a small one because the contact of the stone with your skin will enhance absorption by your body.

Most experienced crystal healers believe in gentle and slow healing rather than a blasting effect. Make your choices sensibly and prudently based on the above three factors.

Other Tips While Choosing Your Crystal

Here are some more tips you can use while choosing your crystal.

Avoid making your choice when you feel mentally or emotionally imbalanced - For example, if you are tired, stressed out, angry, or even excessively happy, don't go shopping for crystals. Wrong ideas likely find their way into your head based on the emotions you are experiencing.

Don't choose crystals for others - As a beginner, completely avoid choosing crystals and gemstones for other people, including your loved ones and close friends. Remember that choosing a crystal has to match an individual's energy vibration with that of the gemstone.

You will not be able to read and decipher someone else's energy vibrations during the initial phases of crystal healing lessons. Even if someone permits you to choose crystals for them, it takes a lot of study and practice, and only the top scholars in the realm can confidently do this work accurately. It is best to keep crystal healing and choosing methods to make choices for yourself alone.

Approach this exercise with an open mind - If you have chosen to access the power of crystals, then it means you are ready to take the plunge without over-analyzing things excessively. If you are looking for 'scientific and logical' proof of every action and thought, you are unlikely to find success. These doubts will color your choice, and you are bound to make mistakes. Therefore, you must approach the exercise of choosing the right crystal with an open mind and trust your intuition to guide you.

Finally, sometimes, despite your best efforts at trying to find a suitable crystal, you realize that you are not drawn to any of the stones that you have come across until now. You don't have to worry about it. Maybe, the time is not yet right for you to connect with the crystals shown to you by the universe through any channel.

If nothing attracts you powerfully, then accept the fact that the time is not yet right for you. Wait and keep your desires alive, and you will find your stone sooner rather than later. Another point of warning is to beware of buying crystals to simply hoard in your house. You run the risk of having stones with energy vibrations unsuitable and even harmful to you.

Holding onto crystals without any purpose or meaning will reduce this exercise to a mere hobby, and crystal healing is more than a hobby. It is a calling. So, listen to your intuition and follow its guiding light. You will never be led astray by your intuition. Believe in its power and leap forward.

And, of course, when you go on your crystal-finding journey, remember to expect the unexpected. You could go in search of finding a lost love, and you could end up finding your true love and realize that the love you lost had a greater purpose than you thought.

Chapter 5:
Purchasing and Caring of Crystals

To choose your crystal, you need to know about crystals and personal zodiac signs. Throughout history, people have been using zodiac stones whether keeping in their home or using it personally. But in today's world, these stones have been replaced with birthstones. There is nothing wrong with it, but using zodiac stones is more appropriate in this case because they have more vibrational energy than using birthstones that have less and are gemstones. Zodiac stones have more reach to your planet per your zodiac sign, and it has more power to support your need, depending upon the kind of stone you use. Of course, it will be about your zodiac sign so that you can amplify your positive characteristics, simultaneously balancing the negative characteristics. Here are the lists of stones with their zodiac signs:

Aries: Blue Tiger's eye, Unakite, Fire Agate, Citrine, Emerald, Bloodstone, Carnelian, Aquamarine, Apache Tears, Aventurine, Amethyst, Clear Quartz, Diamond, and Smoky Quartz

Taurus: Pink Calcite, Onyx, Malachite, Green Aventurine, Amber, Copper, Rutilated Quartz, Selenite, Rose Quartz, Lapis Lazuli, Rhodonite, Emerald, Jape, Blue Tourmaline, and Pink Opal

Cancer: Selenite, Rose Quartz, Ruby, Rhodonite, Red Jasper, Leopardskin Jasper, Moonstone, Citrine, Emerald, Carnelian, Fire Agate, and Sunstone

Leo: Sunstone, Ruby, Pietersite, Mahogany Obsidian, Peridot, Garnet, Amber, Pyrite, Tiger's eye, Howlite, Labradorite, Onyx, Carnelian, Citrine, Amethyst, Yellow Jasper, and Heliodor

Virgo: Sugilite, Sapphire, Snowflake Obsidian, Charoite, Tree Agate, Carnelian, Mookite Jasper, Moss Agate, Chrysocolla, Howlite, Green Aventurine, Amazonite, Amethyst, Hematite, Magnetite, and Sapphire

Libra: Morganite, Moonstone, Mohagany Obsidian, Blue Lace Agate, Blue Tourmaline, Lapis Lazuli, Citrine, Jade, Ametrine, Apatite, Bloodstone, Sapphire, Opal, Pink Tourmaline, Tiger's eyes, and Boulder Opal

Scorpio: Sodalite, Smoky Quartz, Rhodochrosite, Natural Citrine, Red Jasper, Labradorite, Aquamarine, Black Tourmaline, Amethyst, Black Moonstone, and Yellow Topaz

Sagittarius: Labradorite, Blue Lace Agate, Lepidolite, Amethyst, Imperial Topaz, Sodalite, Turquoise, Snowflake Obsidian, Smoky Quartz, Lapis Lazuli, Peridot, Blue Goldstone, Blue Topaz, Black Obsidian, and Jet

Capricorn: Ruby, Emerald, Rainbow Obsidian, Smokey Quartz, Red Tiger's Eye, Onyx, Jet, Malachite, Fluorite, Garnet, Black Tourmaline, and Amber

Aquarius: Larimar, Moonstone, Rainforest Jasper, Garnet, Hematite, Apatite, Aquamarine, Amethyst, Amber, and Angelite

Pisces: Black Tourmaline, Iolite, Turquoise, Ruby in Kyanite, Labradorite, Lapis Lazuli, Fluorite, Jade, Bloodstone, Blue Lace Agate, Amethyst, Blue Quartz, and Aquamarine

To use your stone, you need to know what sort of crystals or stones come into your horoscope and then decide from which stone you want to start your journey. The implementation can be dependent on what your internal body demands. Whether it wants to heal faster from some disease, or whether it wants to get rid of the negative vibrational energies inside it, or both—it's your call. It is better that you spend your time with crystals in a personal space so that you have access to the universal energy source surrounding you. You can recharge with it, or you can rejuvenate. Your personal space where you use your stone can help you in the overall development and provide you with the needed strength to overcome whatever you are looking for. Experiment with each stone. See how they suit you. Trial and error are a must in life, so work yourself with each stone and see what benefits you the most.

The more you touch your stone, the more you utilize its energy. To wear your crystals, you can wear them as jewelry or as regular beauty products. You can put them in your purse or place them in your pockets. The other way you can wear your crystal is to start your day with a crystal layout. For instance, you can place Fluorite to your third eye chakra and amethyst over your heart chakra. If you place these crystals for five minutes before going out to your job, then you will feel an energy shift within you. You can try this with different crystals per your horoscope. You can even use the crystals with your meditation.

With meditation, you can attain your true self, your inner peace. You can dive deeper into your consciousness and can understand the level of your spiritual being. A source for transformation, meditation is best for mind, body, and spirit. Holding different crystals, not at once, but learning to use them at different times, and also not praying to them, is an effective way to enhance your ability to reach a place of quiet stillness. To enhance your abilities with crystals and meditation is to be first comfortable. You don't have to sit in a lotus position. You just have to feel comfortable—just breath in and out. Focusing your attention on breathing will allow you to access the oldest methods of meditation techniques. Be consistent in your meditation. Try using a particular stone for a week or a month and find out thorough tests what your stone is.

To choose the right stone for someone you want to present as a gift. To do that, you need to listen to what your heart is saying. You might be giving crystals to someone for personal growth, healing purposes, or the development of intuition, or it can be any reason. Listen to what your heart says and see which stone you are getting attracted to that you want to give someone. Find that inner knowing. Other ways to choose the right stone to give might depend on the crystal's properties. You might be giving the stone in a gesture that your friendship may get repaired, or the same thing can be said about loving relationships. Knowing the properties of the stone can help you to decide which direction you want to go. You can narrow down your choice with this, shortlisting crystals based on their properties. Or your choice to give the right stone to give to someone might be random. In this case, you have to trust the universe. You might not have any specific choice or the influence of what you should give. Simply spread the various crystals in front of you, or if you are in a crystal shop, in either manifestation, close your eyes. Take a deep breath. Then ask the universe to show you the way to guide you to the highest stone.

You can even combine crystals with crystal therapy. The therapist will recommend different sessions to you depending on your experience with crystals and your progression. Also, depending upon your health, the session will help you to experience detoxification of negative energies. This can help you to discover the underlying surface of your thoughts. The therapist will use different crystals regarding how the different crystals correspond to your body and help you decide your crystal in the therapist's absence when you have to work alone with the crystals.

Another way to choose your crystal is to understand the dynamic between crystals and their color. Scientifically, colors have been linked to affecting human being's emotions and moods. Understanding how the colors of the crystals influence their vibrational energy, you will be able to select crystals based on their healing abilities, how you can balance chakra centers, and create a life toward a more positive journey. For instance, if you are getting irritated by color, you need to work on something to improve your life. If you get attracted, for example, by the color pink, then it means that it is the right time for a new beginning. Another meaning could be that you are empathetic and you need support. You are showing compassion toward somebody. For your emotions to be kept at balance, you need somebody. With the way you see colors and react, you can choose your crystal. The colors of the crystals have their influence on their properties. Below are the colors of crystals and what those colors depict:

Gray: Astral travel, open-mindedness, dream recall, balance, and dream work
Black: Shadow-side work, change, self-reflection, protection, and personal growth
Brown: Nature spirits, inner peace, grounding, stability, and shielding.

Teal: Tranquillity, harmony, inner peace, spirit guides compassion, and portals to angels

White: Meditation, protection, purification, divine connection, and sacredness

Pink: Inner-child work, friendship, compassion, empathy, and new beginnings

Violet: Personal growth, ascension, transformation, conscious awareness, and spirituality

Blue: Justice, wisdom, authenticity, communication, self-expression, truth, and integrity

Indigo: mental expansion, psychic awareness, intuition, and spiritual growth

Yellow: Mental clarity, self-confidence, inner strength, courage, willpower, and bravery

Green: Prosperity, emotional healing, love, physical health, abundance, and compassion, growth

Red: Instinct, motivation, passion, physical healing, vitality, protection, and stability

Orange: inner-parts work, creativity, emotional balance, transformation, sexuality

You can work with a particular color at a time to choose the right crystal for you because a different color indicates its efficiency for specific conditions. Again, trial and error can help you decide what colors to choose and how to heal yourself through positive vibrational frequencies while eliminating the negative ones, working to achieve the balance of mind, body, and soul.

Chapter 6:
Benefits of Crystal Healing

Most people use crystals to relieve the symptoms of pain, stress, and illness. Other gems also can treat conditions such as arthritis, insomnia, depression, and anxiety. Some people undergo regular crystal healing sessions with the use of traditional therapies. Some patients reported increased vitality and increased awareness of mental and physical acuity after undergoing crystal healing.

Specific Crystals with Health Benefits
In addition to the benefits listed above, there are a variety of crystals that are great for treating sick body parts.
These types of crystals include:

Beryl
This stone cleans the throat and helps improve liver function.

Citrine
Promotes blood circulation

Emerald
fights insomnia and provides enough sapphire for sleep-this stone can make your skin healthier.

Topaz
Helps to eliminate varicose veins.

Sodalite
This stone helps raise the normal range of blood pressure.

Some argue that they have experienced a sense of weightlessness as if they have lifted off the ground. On the other hand, others have gone through various energy centers in the body, where they feel tingling and heat. During the session, some people fall asleep or go into deep meditation. Some patients reported feeling even better than before.

Crystal Healing Timeframe

Crystal healing behaves differently depending on the patient and his condition. Some people need to have a single session, while others have advised undergoing weekly crystal healing to experience relief from pain and stress. However, the usual treatment course lasts up to 3 sessions.

The first reference to the use of crystals for medication was found in Papyrus, Egypt. It has written around 1600 BC. For centuries, healing methods using jewels have continued. You can put a healing crystal in your pocket or wear it. You can also crush these crystals into a powder and mix them with the drinking liquid. To get the best benefits of crystal healing, it is essential to choose the right healing crystal that best suits your needs. If you are unfamiliar with this, consult an alternative health care professional.

Below are a variety of healing crystals that you should not miss.

Amethyst

This type of crystal is considered a master healer. It protects and purifies negativity. It also provides a balance between transition states. This stone has a purple color and is associated with the heart chakra. However, not all amethysts are purple. It also has a bluish-red color and is ideal for strengthening the deep mental connection between life's tasks and your inner self.

Chevron amethyst
It helps eliminate karmic patterns and improves spiritual vision and intuition.

Amber
It is known as the softest stone of various types of crystals. It has a calming and relaxing feature. This crystalline healing stone has often used to build a negative tendency while taking the patient's lifeless seriously. Gems have also been used to increase the fidelity of any relationship. Crystal healers see this stone as a form of self-healing. Guide users to have the right feelings. Amber is also devoted to comforting emotions during post-operative problems.

Tiger eye
This is a type of crystal with golden and brown characters. It helps you to be more diligent and focus on what you are doing. This stone has often recommended for students. It also helps improve your mental development. Wearing this crystal will also bring you more blessings.

Jade
This type of crystal is known as a stone of tranquility. Like amber, it also soothes emotions and maintains the peace of the community. This stone can also provide a sense of self-esteem and self-sufficiency. This helps users deal with their situation. In general, jade improves harmony, tranquility, and balance through emotional impatience. As a healing function, it is useful in recovering after painful experiences such as unemployment, funeral, and divorce.

Moonstone
According to crystal experts, moonstone has often associated with enhanced intuition. We also open ourselves to different possibilities. This stone also invites personal change and growth. If you are stubborn and impulsive, Moonstone will be a great help. This sky-blue stone increases concentration and prevents distraction. It has also believed that it can improve one's emotional vision and creativity.

Aquamarine
This stone has been found to calm the nervous system and enhance the user's mood. Most crystal healers believe that aquamarine is also excellent for treating toothache, liver damage, sore throat, and stomach problems. Most sailors prefer to wear this stone for protection.

Quartz
A transparent crystal is an energy conductor and acts as a transmitter and receiver. Having this stone will protect you from harmful external vibrations. This crystal provides harmony and can take good care of your health. Studies show that there are many different types of crystals. Each has its function. Rose quartz is associated with emotions and love. Smoky quartz, on the other hand, is believed to protect the user from negative energy. These crystals are considered the most well-known type. Its transparency gives it a mirror quality that allows you to see things.

Fluorite
This crystal is effective in treating stress. It can also cure infectious diseases and is ideal for fighting viruses. Fluorite restores the skin and helps heal wounds and ulcers. It also regenerates the mucous membranes of the respiratory tract. Blue fluorspar is considered the best crystal for treating nose, throat, eye, and ear problems. Green fluorspar is excellent for stomach disorders, infections, and cramps. Purple and purple fluorspar is best for bone marrow and bone disorders. If you want to release toxins from your body or keep your liver healthy, yellow fluorspar is recommended.

Bloodthirsty
This type of crystal is used for all blood-related problems in the body. This helps detoxify the blood, kidneys, liver, and spleen. This dark green stone with scattered red dots can also improve blood circulation.

Carnelian
Its function is the same as Bloodstone— detoxify the liver and blood. This stone also helps relieve back pain, cramps, and arthritis. It also helps relieve allergic symptoms. Using red and orange rocks as pendants or rings also gives you confidence.

What is the Best Crystal?
There are several types of healing crystals, so you need to choose the right option. Not all crystals are the same. Consult an expert before using any of these crystals. Some healers claim that some gems significantly affect the digestive system, while others are essential for reproductive system recovery. No matter what type of illness you have, there are corresponding healing crystals that adapt to your condition. If you are not aware of this, be sure to consider the above information.

Ever wondered what the real difference is between crystals and minerals? Some argue that they are the same. If you think so, you are wrong. There are vast differences between the two, and recognizing them helps to distinguish them from each other. Defined crystal minerals are considered one of the most important natural resources in the world. They occur naturally in solid chemicals. They have often formed through multiple gemological procedures. Most of them have a very diverse chemical composition. They have highly ordered atom formations with distinct physical properties. In terms of structure, minerals range from pure salts to complex silicates. Crystals, on the other hand, are composed of atoms, molecules, and ions, arranged in a repeating fashion that spans all three spatial dimensions.

Mineral vs. Crystal
Minerals and crystals are not just different in how they have been used. Also, training is different.

Mineral
Minerals fall into two categories
· Non-silicate
· Silicate

Silicate minerals
Silicate minerals are substances that have the basic units of silicate minerals.

Non-silicate
Non-silicates, on the other hand, fall into multiple classes such as sulfides, elements, hydroxides, and carbonates. Silicate-free minerals are scarce compared to silicate ones.

Treating the condition with crystals is not so difficult. However, it does require sufficient time and proper procedures. I hope you get the maximum benefit from them if you use these crystals correctly.

Healing Others with Crystals

Most crystal healers place stones on different parts of the body to improve the patient's soul, mind, and body. You should know how to use these crystals if you intend to help others or even your family.

Make a list of illnesses and complaints from your health clients. Whenever possible, get the crystals you need to solve these specific problems. Then have the patient lie on a flat surface that is convenient for the patient. Turn off the lights and make sure the environment is quiet. Make sure the patient wears loose and comfortable clothes. Then gently place the crystals on the areas of your body that you feel uncomfortable. For sleep problems, soul and forehead-related illnesses put crystals on the chest. Begin meditation in the room while the crystal has overlaid on the human body. Focus on the patient's disease and the power of the crystal. You also need to invite patients to join in meditation together. It has been said that the more mental energy flows through the crystal, the stronger they become. This process is straightforward. I hope that following this process will make your loved one feel better after the session.

Chapter 7:
Healing Chakras with Crystals

The chakras are circular energy vortexes (or sometimes pictured as petalled flowers). They are your life force's focal points or prana – and their states are vital to your holistic well-being.

They affect nerves and major organs, as well as our emotional and spiritual condition. Ideally, all of our chakras should always be in balance, but that's rarely the case.

The Sanskrit word 'Chakra' translates literally to wheel or disc. In Yoga, Ayurveda, and meditation, the term refers to energy wheels all over the mind-body system. Imagine a swirling wheel of energy to visualize a Chakra in your body, which keeps you vibrant, healthy, and alive.

Consider this, why do we face challenges in so many aspects of our lives if we are all energetic beings of limitless potential? Why do our relationships, finances, career, and love life sometimes go awry?

The answer might be that the Chakra that controls this part of your life is dysfunctional, meaning it's your job to strengthen it.

Today, more and more people realize that Chakra Healing's ancient science holds the key to practically everything you've ever wanted in life. Have you ever wondered how certain people might use them?

Becoming a top performer at work almost effortlessly, have all the money they need for necessities and luxuries, and look fabulous while doing so? That's because they are secure in their 1st Chakra, which controls their career and finances.

Do you wonder how people indulge multiple times a week in mind-blowing lovemaking, even when they are swamped and married for years? Most likely, that their 2nd Chakra, which controls their sensuality and passion, is glowing.

Projecting an image of unwavering confidence consistently, even in the toughest situations, and play an active role in their families and communities? That is all thanks to their 3rd Chakra's radiance, which controls their power.

Do people enjoy energetic, caring, and understanding relationships with their teenage kids, partners, co-workers, and friends and settle any conflict in a friendly manner? Their 4th Chakra is undoubtedly healthy, controlling their relations.

Do they always speak their minds, wearing their hearts on their sleeves, and being respected for their authenticity? That's a shiny 5th Chakra at work, which controls the authentic voice.

Do they trust in their "good feelings" to solve problems intuitively at home, make critical decisions at work, and are correct most of the time? They have an efficient 6th Chakra that controls their intuition.

Finally, do they experience an unwavering connection with God and their higher selves and savor the security of knowing that they are watched over? The 7th Chakra, which controls the divine consciousness, is undoubtedly empowered.

The Chakras in Detail

Chakra root, Muladhara root, Red
The root chakra stands for our sense of security and safety.
Location: Spine Foundation
Influences primarily: Your career, mindset of money, and sense of belonging.
Energies: Earth, foundation, emphasis, centralization
Color: Red

You know that when you enjoy your job, your Root Chakra is High, and you get praised for being so good at it. Everybody envies how you make, save, and invest money with your uncanny ability. You will have enough money to go on holiday and buy what you want without feeling guilty. Your friends and family always feel wanted and loved, and when you look in the mirror, you will feel good about yourself, both physically and emotionally.

When you're stuck in an unfulfilled and unrewarding career, your Root Chakra is WEAK or CLOSED, and you never seem to have enough money – which leaves you worried and in debt. Spending money is a frightening experience for you because you question your ability to make successful budgeting. You are suffering from weight or body problems that leave you in your skin, feeling unworthy and uncomfortable.

Chakra Sacra, Svadhisthana, Orange.
The sacral chakra stands for our creativity and our sexuality.
Location: Lower abdomen
Primarily Influences: The source of pleasure in the water.
Energies: Heat, electricity, charging
Color: Orange
Gemstones: Orange gemstones such as carnelian, opal fire, and orange agate fit this Chakra well.

When you see closeness in a positive light as a high, pleasurable, and healthy activity, you know your Sacral Chakra is STRONG. With your partner, you share intense, regular, and lasting lovemaking. Orgasms are mind-blowing, and you and your partner also orgasm at the same time. You make time at least a few times a week to be together, even if you've been attached to the same person for years. You will always attract the right partners – compatible people who feed you, fill you with joy, and make you a better person.

You know that your Sacred Chakra is Low or CLOSED when an intimate thought conjures feelings of remorse and pain in your mind. You may rarely have time or the inclination to make love, and it's lackluster when you do. You and your partner never orgasm simultaneously, and premature or delayed ejaculation is a common problem. You struggle to see yourself as magnetic and also wonder if someone sees you that way. Sometimes, your partners are incorrect for and incompatible with you, and you wonder if you will ever meet "the one."

The Chakra Solar Plexus, Manipura, Yellow.
The Solar chakra Plexus reflects our strength and self-esteem.
Location: On top of the navel.
Your power and channeling ability.
Energies: Fire, water, charging, energy efficiency.
Color: Yellow.
You know that your Power Chakra is STRONG when you are admired for your self-esteem and confidence, both in your career and personal life. You never fear to speak your mind, and you inspire those around you to do likewise. Your family, colleagues, and community see you as a charismatic individual, willing to use your energy and influence to make the world a better place.
Your Power in Chakra is WEAK or CLOSED if you are dealing with self-esteem problems and feelings of indignity. When confronted with critical decisions like moving to another city, changing your career, getting married to your partner, or having children, you tend to question yourself. You feel like one of the world's victims, and you often feel powerless about circumstances and the desires of others. You may also experience frequent stomach pains and worry about your stomach.

The heart chakra, Anahata, Green
The chakra of Heart stands for love and acceptance.
Location: Chest center.
Primary Influences: Love, relationships, and acceptance of oneself.
Energies: Water, soothing, calming, relaxing
Color: Green.
Your friends consider you to be a reliable person. You're perceived at work as the one people your colleagues are comfortable talking to. You feel a sense of heartfelt gratitude for how beautiful your life is and feel compassion for everything around you.
You know that your Heart Chakra is WEAK or CLOSED the moment you tend to sabotage your affection with distrust, anger, and a sense that you will lose your independence if you rely too much on others. You may be struggling with commitment, experiencing frequent fights or misunderstandings with your loved ones, and always remaining "on guard" in case someone is out to hurt you.

Chakra of the Throat, Vishuddha, Blue.
"The Chakra of your "true voice."
The Chakra of the Throat stands for honesty and contact.
Main Influences: The Chakra of the Throat controls self-expression.
Place: The Throat.
Energies: Water, soothing, calming, relaxing
Color: Light Blue.
Gemstones: turquoise, blue apatite, and aquamarine.

You know that your Throat Chakra is STRONG when you are good at expressing your thoughts, ideas, and emotions. You are respected for your determination, excellent communication skills, and willingness to speak the truth, even though some may find it awkward. It enriches your career and your personal life.

You know that your Throat Chakra is WEAK or CLOSED when you always feel that no one cares about your opinions and that you have nothing worth saying. In your professional and social circles, you are likely to be known as the 'quiet one,' and you frequently settle for following others' opinions. Often you experience a blocked and sore throat.

Third Eye Chakra, Ajna, Indigo.
The Chakra of the Third Eye stands for creativity and intuition.
Primary Influences: This Chakra affects your intuition.
Location: Center of the forehead.
Energies: Air, meditative, intuitive, mindfulness.
Color: Indigo.
Gemstones: The most powerful are the indigo gemstones such as iolite and sapphire.
This Chakra acts as a compass within you.
You know that your Intuitive Chakra is STRONG when you can make precise, intuitive decisions and assessments about your career, family, and other people's intentions. You always know things without knowing exactly how you know them, and in everything you do, you have a clear sense of direction and consistency. You may have a vivid picture of where your life is going, and the people around you are likely to count on guidance and advice from you.

You know that your Intuitive Chakra is WEAK or CLOSED when faced with decisions and appeals for justice; you feel lost and helpless. You are indecisive, uncommitted, and unconfident about the choices you end up making, as you have a history of making the wrong ones. You feel spiritually lost and unsure about your real purpose. You often get headaches in your brow region and deal with stress.

Indigo stimulates inner peace, depth, and devotion to emotions.

Crown Chakra, Sahasrara, Violet, or White.
The Crown chakra is an illumination, a spiritual connection, and a connection to our higher selves.
Primary Influences: This chakra influences your source connection.
Location: Top of the head.
Color: Violet or Clear.
Energies: Air, meditative, intuitive, mindfulness.
Gemstones: Use violet or white gemstones such as amethyst, clear quartz, and diamonds for this all-important chakra.

You know that your Crown Chakra is STRONG when you feel connected to a higher power perpetually, be it God, Universal Consciousness, or only your higher self. You are always reminded as you go about your daily life that you are being watched, and you feel immense gratitude for the ultimate love and appreciation you feel for yourself and others. Others call you "gluttonous."

You know that when you feel little or no connection to a higher power, your Crown Chakra is WEAK or CLOSED, and you always feel alone. You feel unworthy of spiritual help and maybe even angry that your higher self might have abandoned you. You often experience migraines and headaches from tension.

Cleansing Crystals

Why do we need our crystals cleaned? There are two reasons; the first is to clean out the physical dirt and polish them into our exciting new crystals. New crystals often have dust on them from sitting in a store or market stall that needs removal. Secondly, you need to remove the energy left on the crystal from other people because many other people probably handled it before you bought the gem.

Ways to make your crystals clean:

1. Breath
When you buy your crystal first, one of the simplest methods of instant cleaning is holding your crystal in your hands and then gently blow your breath on the crystal to clean it. You are adding your life-force energy onto the crystal as you do this, and this will remove and negate all the power left by other people; this will not remove physical dirt and dust.
2. Clean water
You can wash most of the crystals in running water. A word of caution, crystals can dissolve in water; some examples are selenite, kyanite, and azurite, or any of the soft crystals. You can use a damp cloth for these to wipe away the physical dirt. Some books will advise you to use seawater or spring water, but often that is not practical, so use the purest water you can find, with little or no chemicals. It's recommended that you wash the physical dirt from all of your crystals regularly. It is often overlooked if you use the method of cleaning by sunlight or moonlight.
3. Sunlight

Place your crystals in the early morning sun to energize your crystals and cleanse them. A word of caution, when left in the sun too often for too long, gems like amethyst and fluorite will fade. It is also a good idea to use a piece of net to cover your crystals so the birds won't take them.

4. Moonlight

Place your crystal under a full moon outside to infuse moon energy into it. Moon force is a soft feminine energy, so its cleansing is very gentle. It is a wonderful idea to cover them with a piece of net so the animals won't take them at night.

5. Earth Cleansing

Another standard method is burying your natural crystal. Some say that's the only way forward. There are a few precautions with this method, remember where you bury them and do not bury them too deeply. Sometimes you may not find them again as Mother Earth reclaims them. The right way is to keep or conceal them in a pot to be found easily. When you dig them up, you'll need to rinse them off, as they'll have dirt on them.

6. Smudging

White sage has been in use for many years by native cultures for washing and is a compelling way to clean many crystals at once. If you have an extensive collection, putting them out into the moonlight would take you all night. They may be smudged with a white sage smudge stick or white sage incense. Light your stick of incense or smudge, and wave the smoke over your crystals. Sandalwood incense is a good cleanser, too. If you don't like these fragrances, your crystals can be washed with almost any incense. Even you can use resin on a block of charcoal, frankincense, myrrh, or a unique blend of crystal cleaning are good choices. You can close the room door when using resin and charcoal blocks and do the entire room at once.

7. Reiki

When you've been tuned to Reiki, you can use Reiki energy for crystal healing. If you are a level 1 Reiki, hold the crystals in your hands and send Reiki Healing to your gems with intention. Use your Reiki symbols over your crystals for level 2 practitioners, and then send them Reiki.

8. Other Crystals

The amethyst flat clusters are great for putting with other crystals; they will be energetically cleaned just by leaving your jewels on the amethyst for a few hours. Geodes and Transparent Quartz clusters are suitable for use as well.

It doesn't matter which tool you use; remember this is something to do and clean all your crystals regularly, both physically and their energies. Clean them always after healing or after using them.

Chapter 8:
How to use crystals

There are many various ways during which Crystals are often used. This comes right down to personal preference. The more common ways in which Crystals are used are as follows:
Worn on the body (Pendants, Bracelets, and Rings) or the brink of the body (Key Rings or placed in pocket)
• Kept under a pillow
• Used in the bathtub
• In Meditation Practice
• Put around the Home or Offices for space clearing and, of course, for room cleansing
• Counteracting Environmental Pollution
• Making Gem Essences
• Used in Aura Cleansing
• The Laying of Stones on the body for Chakra Balancing
• Worn on or on the brink of the Body

One way to profit from the properties of crystals and stones is to wear them. Often, people who haven't any conscious knowledge of crystal healing will intuitively select crystal jewelry with stones that will have a positive healing effect for them. Crystals worn on or on the brink of the body are often used for healing or protective purposes. These usually do affect the whole body and energy field. The actual location of the stone is additionally conditionally critical in most cases. Placing the stone on or near the precise area associated with the aim of treatment is usually faster. It features a more focused effect; however, as in any healing process, the healing energies will attend where it's intended and to where the healing is required. You'll also direct and focus the energy from the crystal by intention. Sometimes you'll feel that a stone must be somewhere with no pocket or practical place to wear jewelry. Little pouches are often pinned inside clothing for fine-tuned placement.

The length of the chain a pendant is on will help control the strongest effect of the stone. A pendant or necklace resting at the throat chakra may need the best effect on areas governed by the throat chakra (for example, communication and creativity and other throat chakra issues). However, it will still provide energy to the whole aura and human body. A stone worn lower down and almost or on the gut will again have a greater effect on issues and areas governed by the gut's chakra, for example, matters of affection and compassion.

Many people feel that stones worn on the left side need to do with receiving energies, which stones worn on the proper side will primarily influence projective matters and door issues.

Kept under a Pillow

Placing Crystals under the cushion while you are sleeping has numerous advantageous points. Certain Crystals can help with rest issues like a sleeping disorder. They will keep off nightmares and psychic attacks. Other crystals have properties to assist in dream recall, and a few can assist in out-of-body experiences and astral travel.

Used in the bathtub

Crystals are often utilized in the bathtub water or placed around the fringe of the bathtub. This method is extremely effective and enjoyable. Bathing cleanses not just the human body but also cleanses us on all four levels. Bathing can wash away the stresses and strains of the day, any negative emotions we'd be holding onto and may refresh us, soothe us, revitalize us and energize us. Placing Crystals within the bath will absorb any negative energy or emotions.

Additionally, the healing energies of the crystal are going to be directed to where it's intended. Aventurine is an efficient crystal to be used within the bath. Good "all-round" crystals like Clear Quartz, quartz, and Amethyst are also great to be used at bath times.

In Meditation Practice

The energy structure of a crystal naturally imparts stillness and order to the subtle body system, which successively helps to quieten the mind. Problems are issues that haven't yet been resolved by normal thought processes. By altering our way of thinking faraway from everyday issues, an answer can automatically arise. Crystals are often placed in front of you in the meditation practice of they will be held within the hands.
Put around the Home or offices for Space Clearing and your Room Cleansing.

Counteracting Environmental Pollution
Every day our bodies are subjected to harm from everyday substances. This is often referred to as Environmental Stress. Things like plastics, electricity, appliances like radio and microwaves can have harmful effects. These substances increase the strain loading on our systems, making us more vulnerable to illness and disease. The world features a natural electromagnetic field called the geomagnetic field. Man-made substances can reduce this ambient earth energy by shielding it or fixing stronger electromagnetic resonances that will interfere with natural frequencies. Electrical devices within the home and workplace create a strong electromagnetic field around itself. This will cause a drag of entrainment during a one that is run down or susceptible. Entrainment is when the body's natural frequencies become enmeshed with a stronger set of frequencies from an outdoor force. Crystals are often used to amplify personal energy fields, which can counteract the consequences of environmental pollution. The utilization of crystals is becoming quite popular in modern offices where computers, artificial lighting, air-con, metal furniture, and nylon carpets are often disastrous for the energy system.

Making Gem Essences

A Gem Essence may be a liquid sort of crystal energy pattern. Gem Essences are made with water. The unique properties of water make these Gem Essences very effective. Additionally, it is often utilized in ways during which a solid crystal or gemstone can't be used because it's a liquid. Caution should be taken when making Gem Essences as some crystals and minerals are toxic. Always stick with a member of the Quartz family if you're unsure. You'll make Gem Water and Gem Essences. Gem Water is formed by simply placing a crystal gemstone inside a bowl of spring water. The container full of water is then kept until the next day for up to 10 hours.

Gem Water isn't as potent as Gem Essences and is often safely sipped or drank during the day. Gem Water can also be utilized in the bathtub, inhaled, and used as a spray on the body, pets, and even around the home. Gem Essences are made in a slightly different way. They use the energy of sunlight to activate the memory of the water. To form a Gem Essence, you should place the crystal during a bowl and canopy it with only enough spring water to hide the crystal, then place the bowl containing the crystal within the sunlight for about 2 hours. Then half fill a storage bottle with brandy to act as a preservative and fill the remaining half the storage bottle with the Gem Essence. This is often referred to as the mother essence. To form the essence suitable for normal use, you ought to make another bottle known as the stock bottle. You should let the stock bottle contain at least 50% of normal water and at least 50% of brandy. Add a couple of drops of the mother essence from your stock bottle. Again the Gem Essence is often sipped throughout the day. You'll add a couple of drops to the bathtub; it is often inhaled; otherwise, you can use it as a spray on the body, pets, and around the home.

Chapter 9:
Programming methods

Crystal programming has been done in many ways. If you are not familiar with these methods, you need to investigate further.

For a better understanding, these are the different programming methods you should use:

1. Meditation by visualization

Meditation is the usual method of programming a crystal. To do this, you must be sitting in a quiet environment. Next, while grasping the stone, think about the ultimate purpose.

2. Encouraging meditation

It takes a few turns. If you feel you are in a permanent state of meditation, stay focused and blow on your crystal.

3. Meditation with Reiki and other energy technologies

With this method, you can relax and get the crystal. Follow the above methods until the feeling of energy disappears in your hands. Some people believe that after programming the crystal, it will stay in that state for almost 28 days.

The main question is, how do you know that you need to reprogram the crystal? For example, if you planned a transparent quartz group in your room to generate high vibrations, you might need to reschedule that group a few weeks later. However, if everything has been managed in the first week of programming, you can reschedule it in a few weeks.

Common problems and their prescribed crystal

Use a Rhodonite crystal for five days as close as possible to your heart chakra to mitigate the problem of withdrawal.

Abdomen
Lay down and place two smoky quartz crystals, one directly on each side of the stomach and one in the center. Relax and breathe slowly for 20 minutes to relieve pain and pressure.
Scratch
Create a carnelian and obsidian gem elixir, charge it for 1 hour, and tap or moisten this area as many times as you need.

Rich
Make an Emerald Gem Elixir, charge it for 24 hours, and gently spray it on any area of your home, office, or wherever you want to be more abundant in your life.

Abuse problems
Sit in an alternating ring of road crocoite, emerald, and rose quartz. Write down on paper whatever you feel about this situation. Let's continue our life in search of understanding and peace. Fill your role on Mother Earth. Then clean the windows thoroughly.

Receiving
Located in the four corners of a room where you spend most of your time, Charoite creates receptive energy in your life.

Attainment target
Focus on this target while placing the clear crystal with the pointed end directly in front.

Acid Reflux
Use Bloodstone and Smoky Quartz in the pendant to reduce symptoms. Each night, place both stones in the heart chakra for 15 minutes to heal the root cause. Clean thoroughly every night! Acne: Make Amethyst Gem Elixir, charge it for 2 hours, and gently apply this water to your face twice a day.

Active energy problem
To remedy these issues, carry a red jade for five days in the aura field.

ADHD
Wear a green jade bracelet on your dominant wrist and a black onyx anklet on your opposite ankle to balance the energy in your pinna.

Confirmation Mantra
Hold Rhodonite in hand when asserting or mantras every seven days to improve performance.

Positive
Quickly rub blue tourmaline to charge both ends with positive and negative charges. Then focus on the positive end near the problem or offensive person. The positive energy of peace has dispersed, and you feel calm.

Airpower
Bring or wear blue lace agate to enhance the vibration of air energy for seven days.

Air cleaner
Make a clear crystal gem elixir, charge it for 2 hours, and lightly spray it on the air and areas that need purification.

Airplane ear
For pain and pressure in flight, be sure to use a combination of fluorspar and black tourmaline and turn counter-clockwise within 2 inches of your ear until ear pain and stress have reduced.

AKASHIC RECORDS

For easy access to Akashic Records, place five Chinese writing stone crystal grids around you during meditation. Place one in front of your body, one behind, one on each side, and hold the last one in your dominant hand during the session.

Adjustment

Lie down and place the three citrine crystals around your body. Place one on your foot, one on your abdomen, and one on your crown chakra for 15 minutes.

Allergies

Make a carnelian gem elixir, charge it for 2 hours, and lightly spray it all over your body from head to toe three times a day.

Amplification of glass hardening

If you use other crystals in your healing session, use phenacite to amplify the healing effect. For best results, combine the crystals used in that particular session with your phenacite with your dominant hand.

Anal crack

Take a relaxing bath with plenty of carnelians and golden topaz. Please bathe for 10 minutes before bathing. Repeat as many times as you need.

Analytical problems

Wear a purple crystal for five days to see the difference in energy coordination for this issue.

Angel communication

Surround yourself like a little angel during the meditation session and watch the connection improve.

anger
Hold the blue lace agate and breathe slowly and deeply. Feel the wrath of Mother Earth and all the violence that is reborn with positive energy. It takes about 5 minutes to calm down and cool down!

Animal communication
If you use animal communication to improve connectivity, be sure to use Fadden Quartz.

Animal injury
Take the Rose Quartz and place it within a few inches of the animal's injury. Rotate the glass clockwise to remove stagnant negative energy from injury. Note adverse reactions from animals, as they cannot integrate crystal energy as fast as humans.

Animal protection
Attach the Angelite to the animal's crate or collar for extra protection in the energy field.

anxiety
Hold the peridot in your dominant hand and rub it lightly with your thumb. You can also place it on your heart chakra and breathe slowly and deeply. Your anxiety level will decrease in minutes.

Appreciation
To use it yourself, carry or use the Howlite in the energy field for at least three days and make sure the change in energy changes significantly. To tackle the issue of viewing with others, place two people in opposite corners of the room, spending at least 14 days most of the time, and observing behavioral changes.

argument
Take your hematite and hold it gently in your hand during the discussion. Exhale all breath slowly and slowly into hematite. Lower your hand, grasp the hematite with your dominant hand, and relax for a few minutes to soothe any problems that arise.

Grazing problem
Wear or wear emeralds for seven days to address ego problems and arrogance.

arthritis
Make Carnelian Gem Elixir, charge for 3 hours and wash your hands with this water to relieve pain. You can also water the affected area directly.

Ascension
During a meditation session, hold small white spirit quartz, one in each hand, to develop your ascension skills.

positive
If you need to be more proactive to increase vibration levels, such as at work, carry Amazonite with you.

asthma
For those who have asthma, the chain tiger pendant should be low enough to get as close to the lungs as possible. Vibrating energy helps calm the problems you face and reduces attacks.

Removing the astral power cable

Use Variscite when working in an astral power cord removal session. When pulling the power cord, remember to hold it with your dominant hand and use this vibration level of energy to seal the power cord tightly.

Astral projection
Add hematite to the circle around you before beginning the session. Or, once the course starts, hold it in your dominant hand!

Astral journey
Geodes are ideal for work on astral trips and come in various forms, including quartz, amethyst, citrine, and calcite. To address astral travel issues, try to be surrounded by as many geodes as possible during your astral travel session. Make sure they are all from the same crystal. Clear quartz and amethyst are perfect for this purpose.

Athlete's feet
Soak your feet in water with emeralds and smoky quartz. Be sure to clean up the window after each session.

Aura adjustment
During the aura session, citrine is incorporated into the healing to balance energy and align energy with the body.

Aura star
Use Sugilite to absorb the negative energy from your aura field. Remember to clean every day before daily use!

Aura cleaner
During the cleansing session, wear lapis lazuli and walk around the client's aura field to deliver energy, healing tears, holes, stagnant or negative energy. Be sure to clean the glass after the session.

The beginning of the aura
Use rutile quartz during your aura session to create a more open and responsive aura field. Autism: Be sure to place charoite around the area where people with autism spend most of their time calming the problems they face inside.

Car trip
Be sure to keep Moonstone in your car's trunk and glove box when traveling. When traveling on a scooter or motorcycle, be sure to keep it in the passenger compartment.

Consciousness
Wear a Celestine pendant or place it in a common area of your home or office. Besides, wear it during your meditation session to free yourself.

Back issues
For short-term discomfort, lie on your stomach and place three pieces of petrified wood evenly on your back, from the nape of your neck to your bones of your tail. Sleeping for 15 minutes will relieve back pain. If you always have problems, use an inverted pendant so that the petrified wood sits on your back for five consecutive days instead of your chest. The severity of the problem diminishes.

BAD BREATH
Make carnelian and onyx gem elixir, charge for 15 minutes and rinse oral as needed.

Balance of the physical and spiritual world
Take these moldavites at these times and regain the balance between the physical and spiritual worlds.

Locker
A conventional physical balancer is an onyx. Attach this to the pendant around your neck to restore balance throughout your body.

Pressure ulcer
Make a turquoise and black tourmaline gem elixir, charge it for 20 minutes and soak a cotton ball in the tincture. Using a dipped cotton ball, gently tap the pressure sore several times with charged water as needed.

Bedwetting problem
Place the gold topaz on the two opposite corners of the bed frame and the carnelian on the other two different edges of the bed frame to solve the bedwetting problem.

Behavioral issues
For best results with behavioral issues, have the tiger's eye used on the ankle opposite the dominant hand.

Bipolar disorder
Use a combination of turquoise, rose quartz, and onyx to balance the bipolar disorder problem. Turquoise and Rose Quartz are best worn around the wrist or hand, and Onyx are best worn around the ankle for a winning combination.

Bladder problems
With the waist down, place two amber Colors, one on each side of the abdomen. Apply energy and rest for 20 minutes.

Floating
If swelling occurs, lay three golden topaz on their side and place all three in the shape of a triangle on the stomach/abdomen. Make sure one point near the crown chakra and the other two are under the triangle above this. Take a break and relax for 15 minutes. Repeat as necessary, and remember to clean the stone when the session is over.

Ways to utilize healing stones

"There is no correct way [to use crystals]," Askinosie says. All things considered, it's critical to make precious stones a piece of your everyday schedule to receive every one of the rewards.

1. Wear your gems
The more you come in contact with your valuable stones, the more you can take advantage of their vitality, so wearing them is a shrewd procedure. Also, nowadays, precious stones are in truly everything: adornments, magnificence items, apparel, etc. Yet, as a last resort, tucking one into your bra will consistently work.

2. Hurl them into your tote or pocket
On the off chance that wearing gems isn't your thing, or perhaps you simply need to begin little on your gemstone venture, put one in your pocket or satchel. Use it as a touchstone for the day to help ground you.

3. Reflect with them

To up your portion of profound vitality, reflect while holding your precious stones to associate with their magical forces. "You are not imploring the precious stones," Askinosie says. "You're holding them as a hotspot for you to get associated inside yourself."

4. Make a precious stone format

To rationally and vigorously kick off your day right, Askinosie suggests making a precious stone design toward the beginning of your day.

Set down and place a couple of precious stones on your body (i.e., a bit of rose quartz on your heart chakra or an amethyst over your third eye) and simply inhale and marinate in the high-vibe vitality of the stones. "After even only five minutes of laying there, you will feel a move," Askinosie says.

5. Put them in your shower

Make your shower time feel über extravagant by tossing a few pearls in the water. (Not all precious stones are intended to be in the water, so make certain to twofold check first). Askinosie prescribes shungite for detoxing and rose quartz for some sustaining self-esteem.

6. Sprinkle them all through your space

Purging the vitality of your house is as simple as sprinkling a couple of stones all through your space. In addition to the fact that they elevate the vibe, they make for an excellent stylistic layout in each room. Spot a precious stone around your work area to give you great vibes while you work. Utilize a major geode as the focal point on your end table. Or on the other hand, go full scale and make a special raised area with every one of your precious stones, tarot cards, and palo santo.

7. For some profound healing, a precious stone custom may be all together. Askinosie says malachite is a hot stone for a change. "So in case you're prepared to recuperate enthusiastic injuries, pardon yourself or others, or let go of convictions that are never again serving you, load up on the dazzling green pearl, and hold it over your heart for 11 minutes and simply feel," she says.

Now that you have learned so much about Crystal or Precious stones, it is ideal you read about it, get yourself fully informed about Crystal healing and its efficacy. And never fail to practice all that you have learned in this book; it is to guide you through your journey of learning about the spiritual and the healing aspect of crystal. With the right information, you would be successful in life by getting rid of all negative energies with your crystal's help and getting people to love you more. You have already known that there is a different variant of Crystals with different functions.

Chapter 10:
Becoming Conscious of Crystals

Crystal Meditations

Meditation and harnessing the power of crystals can almost be seen to work in synergy. Meditation essentially fills you up with space, emptiness, and awareness. When we are in a meditative space, we are in a state of inner being, heightened awareness, and receptivity. Quantum physicists have found that there is virtually 100% space (99.9 to be exact) within every atom; therefore, the universe is essentially formless! This means that through meditation, we are opening ourselves up to whatever wishes to arise and shine through us for our greatest development. Meditating with crystals can, therefore, have some incredible effects.

Let's look at some of the types of meditation you can include and integrate into daily life. The more you practice and become familiar with these exercises, the more you will develop your unique and intrinsic connection to the crystal kingdom.

Meditation 1: Universal flow

This meditation can have many names. For now, let's call it the Universal flow meditation.

Start by placing your chosen crystal in your left hand with your palm face up but flat. Place your right hand over the top a few centimeters away. This meditation is all about giving and receiving energy, hence the name Universal flow. Your left hand is said to be your receiving hand, while your right hand is the giving. Therefore, placing the crystal on your left palm will allow you to receive its healing energies while simultaneously giving, amplifying your natural healing power.

Take a few deep breaths and close your eyes. Set your intention, thanking the crystal in whichever way feels right for you, and set a short blessing. Now, visualize a beautiful golden light being drawn in through your crown chakra at the top of your head and directly into the crystal through the top of your hand. Take your time. With each breath, visualize and feel this loving healing light energy radiating through your crown, charging the crystal. Due to the power of light energy from your crown chakra and the fact that your crystal will already be cleansed and charged, you should start to feel the effects pretty quickly!

You can stay in this energetic space and breathe golden light into your crystal for as long as you wish. Eventually, you may find you have entered a transcendental state, and depending on the crystal or gemstone, you may begin to receive symbols, insights, or direct wisdom through your higher self.

Meditation 2: Chakra charge

This meditation can be used to charge and clear any of your chakras. To work on all 7 of your main chakras, use clear quartz; otherwise, choose a stone that resonates with you and you wish to connect to. You can also sense which of your chakras may need work, if any, through pendulum dowsing. Set your intention and center yourself, then simply pass the crystal pendulum over each of your chakras. The spiral/circle should inform you of which chakra(s) may need clearing, balancing, or healing. You will feel the energetic state of each chakra just by setting your intention and connecting to the pendulum through energy.

Like in meditation 1, begin by holding your crystal in the top of your left palm with your right hand hovering over. Set your intentions, bless it, and charge it in the same way with the golden light visualization and breaths through your crown. Do this for about 10- 12 breaths. Get in a meditative position and place your right hand underneath your left like a cup with the crystal still on top. Bring your hands and the crystal up to the level of the corresponding chakra and begin to breathe into your hands. Visualize the related color light energy emanating from your hands into the crystal as you breathe, simultaneously feeling sensations within your body. If you have chosen to connect to a heart chakra gemstone to work on your heart chakra, you will visualize a green healing light. The same is for each of the chakras and colors.

With each breath, draw in this healing light energy, both seeing and feeling the swirl around the crystal and your chakra. Synchronize your visual, so the light is embodying both. Once you are in a synergistic flow and feel completely connected to the crystal and the chakra you are healing, project some intentions. The key is to set your intention, project it, and then release it. The process of surrendering and letting go allows your chakra to fill up and the crystal's healing vibrations to be amplified.

Sit with this powerful energy, feeling all the sensations and continuing your breath as you re-charge and heal your chakra. Once inflow, you should begin to receive some visuals or images related to the chakra's energy and may even hear wisdom or guidance being spoken. This is due to the nature of the subconscious and subtle energy. When in this energetic space, you are connected to your subconscious and the consciousness of the crystal and elemental world.

This chakra meditation can be performed for as little as 5-10 minutes for a re-charge and 'quick balance and cleanse' to a fully dedicated self-healing crystal meditation.

Meditation 3: 11 Crystal meditation

This one is a special meditation relating to all 7 of your major chakras. For this one, create a sacred space. It needs to be performed lying down, so make sure you set the tone with the following: minimal/no artificial lighting, candles, soft and healing music such as binaural beats, nature sounds or Tibetan singing bowls and bells, incense, or any other air tool, and some fully charged and programmed crystal water next to you. You will need 7 crystals, each relating to the 7 main chakras, and four quartz crystals. Two will go at the bottom of each foot, a few centimeters apart, and one will be placed in your left hand once the meditation begins. The other will go about 15-20 centimeters above your crown chakra, forming an energetic 'crystal grid.'

This meditation is specifically powerful for releasing energy in the body, which may be stored as trapped or unhealed emotions, traumas, or wounds. It can aid in kundalini flow and balance and clear and harmonize all of the main chakras. It can also help remove any psychic impurities or distortions in your energy field due to both the crystal water and the effect on the etheric body.

Ensure all of your 11 crystals and gemstones have been cleansed, charged, and grounded where necessary and further programmed in a singing bowl or with your intent. Also, make sure the room or space you are in is cleansed through incense, palo santo, sage, or frankincense resin.

This meditation requires you to be in your utmost vibration to truly harness the healing powers of the crystals. It is recommended that you do a short, fast detox leading up to it. This can be a day or two of water and high-vibration foods, such as fruits, vegetables, nuts, and seeds only. It is also essential to be completely knowledgeable and aware of each gemstone's healing properties because when you are lying down in your meditative space, wisdom insight may come to you, which relates to the energy associated with each stone. It is good, therefore, to develop a relationship with each of the gemstones prior.

Once you are lying down with your crystals on your chakras, music playing, and intentions set, the final thing to do is open yourself up to the healing energy. This can be done through an affirmation or intention inside your mind, such as: "I open to receive the healing energy available and wanting to be received. My mind is open, my spirit is welcome, and my heart is strong. I actively open and align my chakras and cleanse my energy bodies. I am safe and protected and connected to the divine. I am ready for deep healing and release and to receive the crystals' consciousness."

The quartz crystal can be held in your left hand during the meditation to receive any energies that wish to come through from the ether. This is because, in this open and subtle connected state, you are not only receiving the crystals' healing powers but are also opened up to new frequencies for other forms of subtle and universal healing to come through. As your left hand is known as the receiving hand, keeping your palm chakras open to receive can lead to increased insight and shifts in vibration. Your right hand should be on either your sacral or heart chakra, as these are the places it sits most comfortably. It can also be moved over each chakra during the meditation, starting at your root and working your way up to your crown to end on either the root or heart. This creates a full circuit with your heart being the center and your root being the foundation, the start of kundalini.

Meditation 4: Being present with crystals

This one is a form of mindfulness and continuous meditation. To feel the crystal world's effects and connect daily to their energies, buy a special gemstone for protection. This can be a pendant, necklace, bracelet, or a combination, or you can buy an individual stone and keep it on you at all times. The key with this is to be in a state of presence and perpetual connection with your chosen crystal or crystals, receiving their healing energy daily and recharging your energy field with metaphysical and spiritual properties. You can also do this as a form of protection from harmful, negative, or destructive energies or to simply keep your vibration high.

You can also make a conscious effort at the start of each day to set your intentions and receive some insight, message, wisdom, or healing experience with crystals. This way, you are forever remaining conscious and connected to the crystal queendom!

Harnessing their Healing Energy

Centering

To harness the healing power of crystals, we must focus on both the center and the ground. Centering brings your awareness to a central space, one where you feel content, comfortable, and relaxed in your body. This allows you to *detach* from all which will not serve you at the moment. Stories, worries, concerns, or stresses, for example, can all dissipate into the infinite when you center, subsequently making your sole focus on your upcoming connection with your crystal.

Not only does centering open you up profoundly for incoming energies, but it also balances your inner energies, encourages chi flow, and opens neural pathways and meridians for information and intuition enhancement.

To center yourself before any crystal connection, be still for a few moments. Bring your awareness inside. Focusing on your breath and then on your subtle energy bodies, visualize your breath traveling down your body and back up again, creating a spiral-like snake. Breathe into this and focus purely on the space and energy inside you and out, no further than your aura. You can end by setting a simple intention for your crystal connection.

Centering can help align you and harmonize your inner systems and chakras, ready for the crystals' effects to take place. You could also center yourself with some crystal water or gem essence!

Grounding

Grounding is essentially connecting to both your lower self and higher self while being centered within. You can ground yourself to become connected to your body, the earth, and the planet as a whole. Grounding greatly aids in connecting to and harnessing crystals' healing qualities.

Follow this short tree meditation to ground you before any crystal connection, meditation, or healing exercise. Simultaneously, if you don't have access to nature or it is not the right time or space, connect to flower essences, herbs, or plants and flowers in some way. They have a deeply grounding influence and can help you feel at one with yourself and the world while raising your vibration.

Tree meditation for grounding

Find a quiet or comfortable place outside. Choose a tree that resonates with you. Sit down with your knees bent, feet flat on the earth, and back straight, gently resting against the tree's trunk. This grounding meditation is best performed barefoot as it is through your feet chakras (one of the less known chakras) where your chi and subtle energy connect to the earth.

Start with 10- 12 conscious breaths and close your eyes. Bring your awareness inside and then to the tree. The key with this exercise is to be mindful of your connection to the tree; to mother nature. The tree's roots symbolize your feet, the trunk, your spine, and the leaves, your crown chakra, the invisible streams of consciousness rising above your head. Once you feel centered within, begin to visualize a loving but gentle golden light traveling through your feet, up to your spine, and the top of your head with each breath. Simultaneously imagine the route back down with each breath out. Once you are in a steady flow and are fully connected to your body and all the physical sensations, imagine the same golden light traveling up the tree's trunk through the roots to the top of the leaves and back down. Synchronize your breath to the trees.

After a while, you should start to feel your and the tree's heartbeat as one. You may even feel a strong swirl of energy emanating from your back as if the tree is communicating with you.

Although not all crystals are for connecting to the earth, and some are for doing the opposite, this grounding exercise is very beneficial to increase the effects of any crystal healing connection. It will raise your inner vibration, opening your energy field up to the powers of the crystal world.

Many people around the world have learned how to harness their healing energy for themselves and others. Experienced crystal healers and therapists can read auras, provide full-body crystal treatments, balance and heal chakras through chakra clearing with crystals, and scry (receive information, wisdom, and guidance from crystal balls). In Atlantean times, it is believed that the ancients were existing at a much higher frequency than many of us humans today, and this was due to their deep understanding and use of crystals.

Crystals have essentially been used all over the world and for thousands of years. If you wish to expand your understanding and connection to crystals after reading the exercises, you can look into crystal healing or therapy courses near you and train to become a professional crystal healer. You can also see any practitioners or therapists in your area or meet-ups with like-minded people waking up to the power of special gemstones. Harnessing and connecting to the energy of crystals is not exclusively for you in your home - there are lots of people who share in your crystal magical 'madness!'

Aura Strengthening and Protecting, and Vibration-Raising Exercises

Tied in closely with crystals and their powers is aura strengthening and protecting exercises. As you are aware, crystals work through the subtle energetic bodies and layers of existence. The human aura, otherwise known as the electromagnetic energy field, interacts with the crystals' electromagnetic energy field, leading to profound change and transformation. As it is through the aura and the etheric body where most crystal healing occurs, it is essential to engage in regular exercises and activities to strengthen it and shield yourself from negative or harmful energy.

Aura Protecting: Developing your Third eye and Psychic abilities

The third eye and all aspects relating to psychic and intuitive abilities connect strongly to the aura and the ability to protect yourself. This is because protecting yourself is not just physical. We can protect ourselves mentally, emotionally, and spiritually through the *power of our minds*. As all subtle bodies are linked, strengthening the mind is essentially strengthening the aura. Connecting to gemstones specifically for the third eye and subtle and psychic perception can aid significantly in this.

Try the exercise below with any of the following crystals: amethyst, lapis lazuli, azurite, celestite, or clear quartz.

Mentally construct a protective pyramid around you. Begin by getting into your meditative space, following the breath, inner awareness, and going within the sequence. Also, remember to cleanse and charge your crystal properly. A pyramid is highly significant when working with the third eye and auric field strengthening due to its inherent energetic association. The pyramid is the three, the holy trinity. The pyramids of Giza were created based on ancient knowledge regarding sacred geometry, as were other temple-pyramids around the world. Just like colors carry a unique frequency, so do shapes.

The key to this exercise is to combine visualization, inner knowing, and transcendental meditation with strong intentions. Once you are in inner calm and space, bring your chosen crystal up to your third eye. Begin by lightly tapping it against your brow chakra, visualizing healing and enhancing energy sparking from the crystal. Then gently rub it in circular motions against your brow/third eye. Remember to feel and connect on an inner level. You need to remain aware of what is happening inside the subtle realms of existence to experience this effect.

You can program and project intentions into the crystal while rubbing it against your brow. Essentially you are activating your psychic center through the stimulation and connection of the crystal.

This exercise is simple yet highly effective at strengthening your mental abilities and shielding you from psychic attack. It can act as protection and increase your ability to perceive subtle energy, further boosting your auric field.

Aura strengthening: Developing your Intuition

Strengthening your intuition will also aid in your auric field protection due to the mind-body-spirit connection. Working with crystals that enhance intuition is the best way to do so, and so is combining meditation exercises and engaging in healthy and regular cleanses. Detoxifying your system with crystal water can help relieve you of any psychic impurities and simultaneously strengthen your auric field.

Use the Universal flow meditation exercise in 'Crystal Meditations,' however, adapt it, so it is specifically intended to charge you with evolved intuitive abilities. While in the energetic space of connection and synergy with your crystal, visualize your aura expanding. As you see and feel your aura expanding, imagine it merging with the crystal's auric field, as if it is wrapping you in a loving hug.

Raising your Vibration

This technique can be used to build a protective circuit around you while raising your vibration profoundly. You can be seated on a chair, crossed-legged in a meditative position, or lying down. A quartz crystal is ideal.

Begin by bringing a white light down through your crown chakra. Do this with your mind and your breath. Anchor yourself to mother earth by grounding your energies with her, visualizing strong roots growing from your feet, and merging with the piles of earth.

These roots can be literal or visual, i.e., you can picture them as real, earthy brown roots or as a celestial type light. Next, visualize warm pink energy coming up through the earth and your feet into your heart chakra. This energy embodies unconditional love.

Shift your awareness back to the white light, now filling your entire body. Watch the pink merge and dissolve into the white, removing all impurities, negativity, and distortions as it does. Now visualize a golden or white light emanating from your quartz in your hands. Visualize it going up through the center of your spine, up to your chakras, and residing in your crown.

Breathe into your crystal to fill it with unconditional love. Connect and tune into this energy, finally creating a sphere in your mind starting from the crystal and circling all around you in a protective shield. Stay inside this sphere, focusing on all the various sensations.

This exercise is very powerful at raising your inner vibration, grounding and balancing your chakras, and centering yourself. It can naturally bring an evolved sense of intuition and psychic sight and create strong feelings of love, acceptance, and connection to your inner being and the divine.

Dispelling Negative Energy

This technique should only be attempted once you have become familiar with crystals and their power and engaged in activities to connect with them and raise your inner vibration. Dispelling is drawing out negative or harmful energy and getting rid of it. It can only be performed with a Clear Quartz crystal (or Selenite wand, however, for now, let's stick with Clear Quartz!) and is advised to do once you have worked on aura strengthening and protecting exercises.

To begin, you should first perform some centering, grounding, or vibration raising activity, or all three if possible. Dispelling effectively clears the aura and etheric field, healing and unblocking negative energy from the chakras and removing any negative energy that may be lingering.

Start by creating a connection with your crystal. This can be done through meditation or through simply closing your eyes and setting your intention. Hold your clear quartz in your left palm with your right hand over the top, like in Universal flow meditation. Take 3- 5 deep breaths and say some intentions into your crystal. These can include "thank you for your healing energy, I open up to your healing power" or "I charge you with love, light, and truth and open myself up as a channel to dispel and clear any negative energy from my energy field."

As your right hand is the giving hand and your left is the receiving, hold the crystal in your left hand with the point facing outwards. You don't need to grip too tightly, but just comfortably and with intention. Sit down in a meditative position and point the Clear Quartz towards one of the energy centers you feel has become blocked or polluted with other people's energy, harmful thoughts, or delusions. This will most likely be your sacral chakra where emotions pass through and are stored, your heart- if your authentic nature of kindness, love, and compassion has become clouded or your throat responsible for communication and the ability to express yourself. It may also be your third eye or brow relating to your ability to perceive and connect to higher levels of thought and awareness.

Now point the end towards your chosen chakra, and make a brief physical connection. Hold out your right arm straight by your side with your palm flat facing outwards, as if you were imitating a dance, yogic, or freedom pose. The key is to have the palm of your right hand facing upwards and away from you. With your intention, draw out the negative or blocked energy from your subtle body. You can do this by visualizing a stream of pure golden light physically drawing out the energy and can combine it with conscious breathing. Be strong in your mind and your intention, yet don't over force. Force is necessary, though.

Once you can begin to feel a tingling sensation or feel a shift occurring in your chakra, crystal, and left hand, send an intention to your right. *Create the circuit* in your mind, from the golden light drawing out the harmful energy, traveling through the crystal, into your left hand, and straight out into your right. It should not stay in your body. You are merely a channel and do not wish to embody or hold onto this energy. Send it straight to your right hand and watch it dispel into the ether around.

At this stage, you may feel intuitive to do a few forcefully gentle and abrupt arm jolts or move your hand outwards in a flowing motion. Essentially your right hand- which gives universal energy- is giving the negative energy from your body over to the ethereal realms. It is here where it is being dispelled and no longer causing you harm.

This may last from 5 minutes to around 15 or 20, depending on how strong the energy flow is. Remember to end with an intention setting and closing the current. Your crystal should be cleansed and recharged after this and some grounding and centering performed on yourself. You may even feel a 'spark' in your palms.

Chapter 11:
Recommended Crystals for Beginners

Each crystal has a vibrational force that works to attract different energies to our lives. Sometimes these energies are positive and help to heal us from the detrimental effects of negativity. Other times these energies are used to open us up to creativity, wealth, love, passion, relaxation, motivation, and more. It should immediately be clear why we would want to bring these energies into our lives, but it is helpful to do it in a way in which you don't overwhelm yourself. This might be a little bit confusing to understand, so let's turn to a metaphor.

Ninety percent of the adult population in North America drink coffee, so let's use this as a jumping-off point. If you prefer, pretend that we are talking about alcohol or beer, as these follow the same pattern as coffee. When you are first introduced to this delicious beverage, it can be quite overwhelming. A single cup can keep you up all hours of the night, and you may even experience muscle spasms. If you haven't had any coffee before, you don't want to start with an espresso. But, if you have been drinking coffee for any length of time, then you know how quickly you get used to it. Then you can start drinking extra-strong or even espresso if you want. It will still have a much stronger kick than a regular cup of coffee, but it won't knock your socks off anymore. This is pretty much exactly what happens when we start using crystals. Those that are too powerful can be overwhelming and put us off using crystals, just like an espresso taken early can make us not want to try coffee ever again. When you build up naturally, you increase your ability to handle even the strongest crystals' energies.

You may want to go ahead and grab yourself a strong crystal such as almandine garnet, but you will find your experience to be far more pleasant if you take your time and build up your skill. It is better to build slowly than to burn out quickly, after all!

Hematite

Hematite is used to promote a sense of stability within our emotions. Instead of being all over the place, with our emotions scattered to the winds, hematite helps us to find an island inside ourselves from which we can identify and witness our emotions. From this place, we can take much-needed calming breaths that help us remove negativity from our lives. Things like stress and anxiety can be let go of, and the hematite will trap them inside of itself, preventing them from returning to you.

The relaxation that hematite offers make it a wonderful stone for those who feel like they are often under a lot of pressure. If you are a university student or someone working in a hectic industry, a piece of hematite should be kept nearby to remind you that you are more than your studies or your job. Even though there may be inevitable stresses, they shouldn't be allowed to ruin your mental and spiritual health.

Hematite has a gentle aura, which is ideal for beginners, as it creates a soothing feeling rather than a strong or overpowering one. It needs to be purified regularly to remove the toxic and negative energies that it absorbs. I believe that beginners should always have at least one crystal that requires them to perform a cleansing, as this is a crucial process and should be learned early. Many of the more advanced crystals you will come to use need to be cleaned quite often; otherwise, they can backfire and invite more negativity than they remove. Starting with a gentle stone like hematite will allow you to get used to cleansing without increasing the stakes in a large way. The more you can learn at this point, the better off you will be in the long run.

Citrine

We've seen citrine pop up several times throughout this book, and so it should be clear that this is one crystal that is extremely flexible in its uses. It can help you stay motivated, it can help you stay positive, it removes negative energy from your life, and it is even used to help attract wealth. Not only that, but it also has connections to fertility and creativity. With all of these disparate features, you might think that this crystal would be overly powerful.

And yet citrine is anything but. While it has an extensive range of possible uses and attracts lots of different energies, citrine is a very mild crystal with a subtle vibrational energy that makes it easy to use. If you could only select one crystal to begin with, you would be well advised to go with a piece of citrine.

Blue Lace Agate

We've looked at red agate, but if you are going, to begin with, any type of agate, then it should be one of the blue lace varieties. This crystal has a smooth texture and a light blue color that promotes a sense of calm. Blue lace agate is one of the crystals for beginners that helps heal this divide and reconnect us to that self-deep inside. It also helps us speak more openly and sincerely, both to ourselves and in our interactions with others.

Blue lace agate is among the best crystals to wear in a necklace, as it is usually strongly tied to the chakra in our throat that helps facilitate communication. If you are in a position in which you need to be a leader, or perhaps even just a public speaker, then a piece of blue lace agate was worn around the neck can help keep you speaking clearly and expressing nothing but your deepest truth.

Clear Quartz

Among the many quartz crystals that we use for healing purposes, clear quartz is one of the strongest and yet one of the best for beginners. Called the Master Healer, clear quartz is used to help us repair the damage from negativity, keep our aura clear from darkness, release negative emotions that have caused us pain, and even more. It is also one of the crystals which absorb negativity into itself so that it can't re-enter your life. What that means is you will need to learn to practice cleansing rituals to keep your clear quartz working at the highest level possible.

Clear quartz also acts as an amplifier. While it doesn't have a strong energy of its own, or, rather, intrusive energy, clear quartz helps boost the crystals' vibrations around it. If used in a spread or a ritual, this can cause another weaker crystal to become much stronger. This is something that beginners need to be aware of. You may be using blue lace agate, for example, because it has a subtle power that makes it terrific for beginners, only to find that it becomes much more difficult to use once clear quartz is introduced. To address this, begin by using clear quartz on its own, and then slowly introduce other crystals into your practice, whether that be meditation, wearing crystal jewelry, or creating a crystal grid. It is always best to build up and introduce new crystals one at a time to feel the difference and not overwhelm yourself in the process.

Amethyst

When you feel swamped by life, the crystal you use to help relax and ground you must not be itself overwhelming. This would only exacerbate the problem rather than help to solve it. Thankfully, amethyst is one of the best crystals for clearing the mind, plus one that is a great choice for beginners because of the gentle vibrations it emits. Amethyst also has protective properties that it uses to ward off negative energy that would otherwise seek to keep you down.

Meditation with amethyst will clear the mind and help boost our spiritual defenses. It can also be used in a grid, though it is important not to add too many crystals to a grid at once when you are beginning. Perhaps the most beneficial aspect of amethyst is how it helps to protect us in our sleep. Negative energies often try to get at us through our subconscious, and we see this manifest itself as nightmares. These can prevent us from getting refreshing sleep or sometimes wake us up in the middle of the night. To prevent these negative energies from disturbing our rest, place a piece of amethyst under your pillow before bed so that you can benefit from the protection it offers.

Pyrite

Known as fool's gold, pyrite is used to promote wealth and success in business. Keeping a piece of pyrite at your workspace can help you achieve more, get a promotion, and invite healthy energy into the workspace. This place may typically have a problem with attracting positivity. Another of the benefits that pyrite offers is a deep sense of confidence, which is fantastic for those that need to assert themselves in their jobs.

Where some crystals have a strong energy that can be overwhelming, pyrite has a strong energy that helps to improve your willpower. If you find yourself unable to get motivated or to push through work and deal with the other tasks you have on your plate, meditating with pyrite and keeping it nearby will help you overcome these challenges.

Chapter 12:
Frequently asked questions

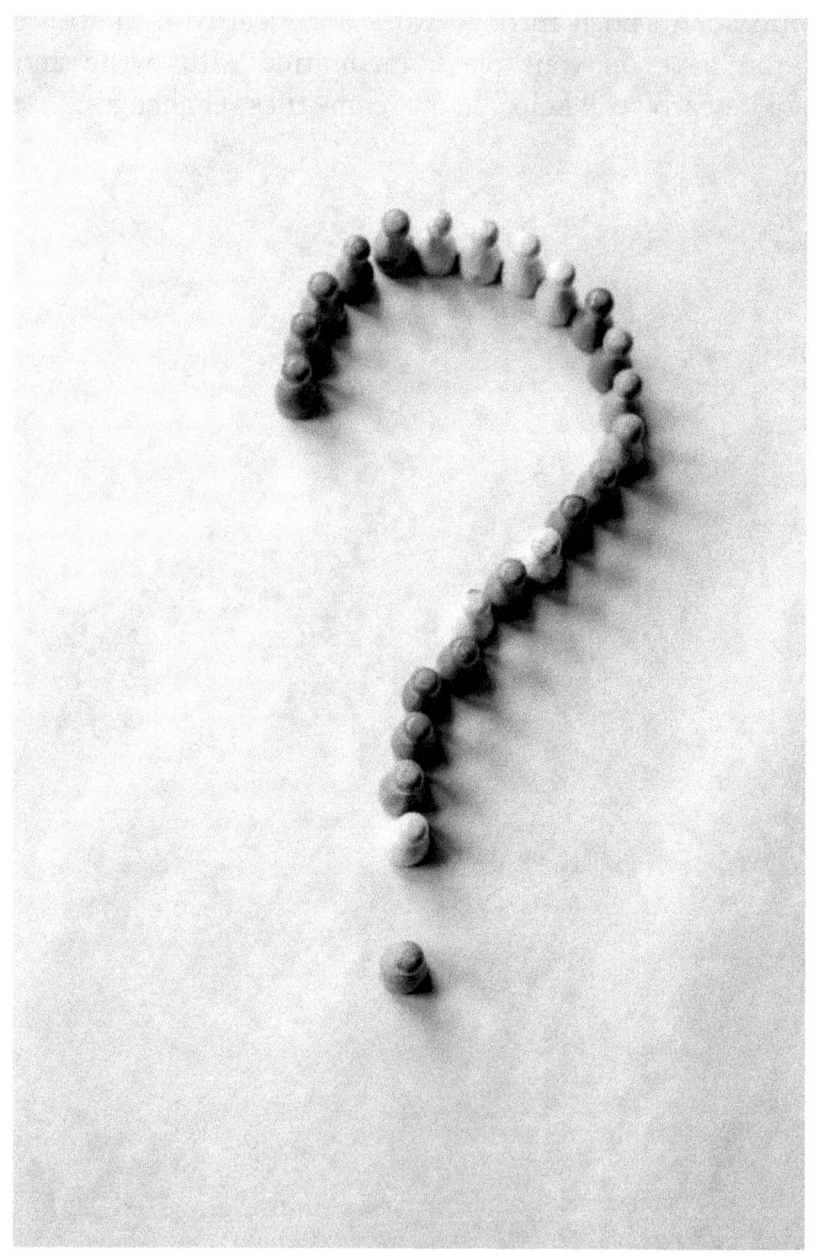

Now that you know about crystals in-depth, here are a few questions that require answers.

How to buy the stones from a trusted buyer?

There are many crystals in the market. Identifying the real ones from the fake ones is difficult. Hence, it is encouraged to read a book about crystals such as this. Knowing crystals will help you when you buy stones. Buying crystals from authentic stores that display crystals as what they are can help you to make a better choice. Some crystal sellers will try to sell you fake products, but don't be afraid. Question every merchant who sells crystals until you are satisfied and get your money's worth.

Can you use crystals instead of using professional healthcare?

The answer is simply no. Yes, it is better to try alternative ways, but avoiding the real science with evidence is not the way for crystal cures too. Yes, crystals possess healing properties, but they cannot replace the modern healthcare system. Again, crystals cannot be replaced with medicine and drugs.

Can you just pick up any crystal you like and use it?

You must understand the difference between crystals and stones. The best thing to know about the crystals is to just simply increase your knowledge, as said before. Know about its nature, its healing and physical properties. Don't use random crystals. They can be harmful too because some of them contain the toxin. Yes, it is right to go with your intuition, but have some knowledge first. Also, when you make crystal water, be careful there. Expand on your knowledge before you try anything.

Which are the good stones—raw or polished?

If you get an original stone: unpolished or uncut, use them because they are original and carry a higher vibrational frequency. On the other hand, there is nothing wrong with polished crystals too. And also, it is a matter of choice. For example, if you use original Selenite, they easily break while imitating the reflection of rubbles whenever you touch them, so it is better to work with polished Selenite.

Are crystals recognized for their healing role in the world?

Crystals can be easily located all around the world these days. It also tells how widespread they are. Crystals are also a huge part of some cultures. Their historical significance is remarkable. You can even order crystals online.

Does size matter in crystals?

The simple answer is yes. Bigger crystals have more vibrational frequencies than smaller ones. But this doesn't mean that smaller stones do not have any power. They can be utilized in so many ways. From using them for jewelry to carrying them in the pocket, you can find ways to keep them closer to you than bigger crystals. Yet they are also available in a bigger size, as tall as six feet, but you can't utilize them in many ways.

What if there is someone who doesn't believe in crystals? Do the crystals work for them?

Crystals carry vibration. They can feel your vibration, can connect with them. They know what you feel. If you do not believe in them, they will not work for you. You need to feel them and absorb their energy. When you do not open your door, they do not open their door for you. For people who want to receive their vibration for healing, the doors are open for them. If you do not believe in them, find some other healing ways.

What does it usually mean when someone gets attracted to a crystal?

It usually means that that crystal is for you. For some people, crystals come into their life out of nowhere. It is like their circumstances want that particular crystal so that it can heal them. When you go to a store, you can hold the different crystals, each one in your hand. See how you feel with them and to which you are getting attracted.

Once you buy a crystal, what should you do with them?

Whenever you make your first purchase, soak the crystals in saltwater to eliminate the negative energies that they have picked up in the store. Then you can put those crystals in sunlight for recharge. Use the crystals by holding them to set your intentions in them, such as the mantras described in this book.

Are crystals too expensive?

The simple answer is no. And it depends on you. The cost of the crystal depends on the kind of stone and its origin. There are usually three types of crystals, and their prices differ. They are raw stones, cut stones, and tumble stones. Raw stones don't contain a shine, but they carry strong vibration, whereas cut stones are a lookalike of gemstones and are polished. You can wear them as jewelry. On the other hand, tumble stones are available easily. You don't need to spend a lot on them.

Do crystals have an expiry date?

No, but recharge them with sunlight, or use them under a full moon. They may not get expired, but they may get out of touch, so connect them with mother nature.

Conclusion

Crystals have been admired for thousands of years, in every part of the world, for their beauty and strength.

Yet, in the modern era, when our heads start spinning, many of us look back to those ancient ways to release fear and embrace some grounding energy.

Crystal is called a healing stone of heart, health, and good fortune. It comforts and heals blows to the heart that we can open up to feel worthwhile and receive experiences that go beyond our wildest dreams. "It is an excellent stone for anyone seeking peace or moving up in their careers.

The great thing about crystals is they're indiscriminate in their energies. Thus, even if your spiritual side is not healthy or a large part of your day-to-day life, you will enjoy the benefits of healing gems, whether you wear them as jewelry, meditate with them, or place them as home decoration.

Often, it is the energies of individual crystals that call us that make our choices to use the healing crystal so effortlessly – as long as we allow our intuition to guide us.

Just remember crystals are no magic fix. It's all about your energy and improving the work and endeavors you're already doing. If you are open to their healing powers, you are halfway up there already. My wish is for you to experience peace like no other with this knowledge you have gotten; you have a peaceful life free of all negative energy.

Start collecting, have fun, and let those positive vibes flow.

www.ingramcontent.com/pod-product-compliance
Lightning Source LLC
Chambersburg PA
CBHW050506120526
44588CB00044B/1575